Asif Khan

W0038269

Writer: *Combustion*, selected as one of six new plays for the Arcola Theatre's playWROUGHT #2 Festival, 2014. Progressed through to the final stage of the BBC Writers Room Script Room 8 Scheme. *Tight Bastards*, reading at the Soho Theatre for Tamasha Theatre (2015) and at Theatre 503 (2016). *Willkommen*, commissioned by Tamasha & The Migration Museum. *The Plot*, reading at the Soho Theatre for New Muslim Voices (2016), commissioned by Tamasha. Member of Tamasha Playwrights Group & BBC Comedy Room.

Awards: RADA – Won a Laurence Olivier Bursary Award & Sir Alec Guinness Memorial Award.

Snookered – Nominated for 'Best New Play' & 'Best Ensemble Cast', Off West End Theatre Awards 2012. Won 'Best New Play' at the Manchester Theatre Awards, 2013.

Plot to Bring Down Britain's Planes – BAFTA Winner, 2013

Adopt a Playwright Award (OffWestEnd) – Nominated and made it through to the final shortlist.

Love, Bombs & Apples – Nominated as a finalist for Best Stage Production at the Asian Media Awards 2016 and Nominated as a finalist for Best Stage Production at Eastern Eye Arts, Culture & Theatre Awards 2017.

BBC New Talent Hotlist 2017 for New Writers.

Nominated as a finalist for Best Actor at Eastern Eye Arts, Culture & Theatre Awards 2017.

Beam Awards 2017 – Nominated for The Male Actor of the Year Award.

www.theasifkhan.com

First published in the UK in 2017 by Aurora Metro Publications Ltd
67 Grove Avenue, Twickenham, TW1 4HX
www.aurorametro.com   info@aurorametro.com

Combustion © copyright 2013 Asif Khan
Cover design © copyright 2017 feastcreative.com

Production: Simon Smith

With many thanks to: Ivett Saliba and Claire Alejo.

All rights are strictly reserved.

For rights enquiries including performing rights, please contact the publisher: rights@aurorametro.com

No part of this publication may be reproduced, stored in or introduced into a retrieval system, or transmitted in any form, or by any means (electronic, mechanical, photocopying, recording or otherwise) without the prior permission of the publisher. Any person who does any unauthorised act in relation to this publication may be liable to criminal prosecution and civil claims for damages.

In accordance with Section 78 of the Copyright, Designs and Patents Act 1988, Asif Khan asserts his moral rights to be identified as the author of the above work.

This paperback is sold subject to the condition that it shall not, by way of trade or otherwise, be lent, resold, hired out, or otherwise circulated without the publisher's prior consent in any form of binding or cover other than that in which it is published and without a similar condition being imposed on the subsequent purchaser.

Printed by 4edge Limited, UK.
ISBNs:
978-1-911501-91-6 (print)
978-1-911501-92-3 (ebook)

COMBUSTION

by

ASIF KHAN

AURORA METRO BOOKS

For my dear friend Zenab Khan.

2nd July 1976–3rd July 2014

CONTENTS

About AIK Productions

AIK Productions was created by Asif Khan in 2015 to produce new, high quality theatre specializing in stories and voices from minority backgrounds.

Its first production in 2015 was *Love, Bombs & Apples* by award-winning playwright Hassan Abdulrazzak. It had a sold out run at the Arcola Theatre as part of the Shubbak Arab Arts Festival in 2015. The show returned in 2016 for four weeks at the Arcola Theatre alongside a UK tour to: Northern Stage (Newcastle), Mercury Theatre (Colchester), Printers Playhouse (Eastbourne), Attenborough Arts Centre (Leicester), Cast (Doncaster), York Theatre Royal (York), Theatre in the Mill (Bradford), Oldham Coliseum (Oldham), Kinara Festival (Ace Centre, Nelson) and Arabica Arts Festival (Liverpool).

It was nominated for Best Stage Production at the Asian Media Awards 2016 and as a finalist for Best Stage Production at Eastern Eye Arts, Culture & Theatre Awards 2017.

"**** Bubbling humour... Quartet of monologues with a profound ability to find humour in the most over-trodden tragedies" – *The Stage*

"**** Searingly satirical... brilliantly observed" – *LondonTheatre1*

"**** Powerful, political theatre... Laugh-out-loud moments... Chris Morris' hilarious film, *Four Lions*, sprung to mind" – *Hackney Gazette*

"**** Invigorating... inspiring... exhilarating... Rosamunde Hutt's economic, elegant single-room production transports us effortlessly to each milieu, as does Khan's extraordinary gift for transformation" – Carole Woddis

@AIK_Productions

About Tara Arts

Tara Arts are established as one of the UK's foremost creators of cross-cultural theatre. Tara Arts' work consistently seeks to connect worlds, through new writing and reimagined classics. Tara Arts was founded in 1977 and will celebrate its 40th anniversary in 2017.

In September 2016 after extensive renovation, Tara Theatre was opened in Earlsfield, south west London by the Major of London, Sadiq Khan. This award-winning theatre – the country's first dedicated multicultural theatre – was designed by architects AEDAS Arts Team.

Tara brings together artists and their audiences under the shade of our tree. All are welcome to step through the antique Indian doors into a world of colour where the small is global.

With its unique earth stage floor, Tara Theatre's 100 plush seats offer an intimate setting to appreciate actors weaving their magic. Its studio space provides opportunities for rehearsals and workshops, small events and meetings, while its outdoor patio garden – flanked by railway sleepers – offers a haven from the hustle and bustle of a busy urban high street.

Winner of The Stage Award for Sustainability in 2017, Tara Theatre is home to connecting worlds.

Patrons: Sir Richard Eyre CBE, Shobana Jeyasingh MBE, Naseem Khan CBE, Hanif Kureishi CBE, Sir Salman Rushdie and Nitin Sawhney.

Founders: Praveen Bahl, Ovais Kadri, Sunil Saggar, Vijay Shaunak and Jatinder Verma MBE.

www.tara-arts.com

@Tara_Arts

8

For Tara Arts

Artistic Director   Jatinder Verma
Executive Director   Laurie Miller-Zutshi
Associate Producer   Jonathan Kennedy
Associate Director   Claudia Mayer
Head of Finance   Julia Brundell
General Manager   Alexandra Wyatt
Technical & Operations Manager   Tom Kingdon
Finance Manager   Xiao Hong (Sharon) Zhang
Digital Marketing Coordinator   Katie Robson
Development Assistant   Lauren Harbord
IT Consultant   Hitesh Chauhan
Welcome Team   Battersea Arts Centre
Volunteer Ushers Team

Tara Arts Makers and Mentors

Ausaf Abbas, Adrian Mayer, Dennis Mountford, the Shinebourne family and Elisabeth Smith.

With thanks to

The Carne Trust, Arts Council England, Royal Victoria Hall Foundation, White Light, Arcola Theatre, Tamasha Theatre, RADA, Robin Soans, Carl Miller, Nick Connaughton, Sheena Patel, Peter Singh, Jaz Deol, Michael Luxton, Muzz Khan, Nic Wass, Fin Kennedy, Dane Millard, Earlsfield Car Maintenance Centre (ECMC), the Ziaulla family and the Khan family.

Introduction

It could have been a poster for *Combustion*: Saffiyah Khan confronting an incensed EDL supporter at a demonstration in Birmingham city centre on Saturday 8th April 2017. The fact that it went viral and that she got many thousands of responses in support of her action – which was in turn in support of a young Muslim woman wearing the hijab, Saira Zafar – is a very positive and hopeful news story in amongst the tide of negative ones which induce fear and inspire hatred. Asif Khan's play is a much needed insight into a world which is largely unknown to those who are not part of or closely related to it. It raises issues that are complicated, difficult, and in need of greater exposure, knowledge and understanding; Asif's writing confronts these issues directly with humour, empathy and grace.

Nona Shepphard, Director

April 2017

Asif Khan – Writer & Co-Producer

Asif trained as an actor at RADA. His theatre work includes: *The Hypocrite* (RSC / HullTruck), *Paradise of the Assassins* (Tara Arts), *Love, Bombs & Apples* (Arcola & UK Tour), *Handbagged* (UK Tour, Tricycle Theatre / Eleanor Lloyd Productions), *Multitudes* (Tricycle Theatre), *Queen of the Nile* (HullTruck), *Kabaddi Kabaddi Kabaddi* (Arcola Theatre), *Snookered* (Tamasha / Bush Theatre), *Mixed Up North* (Out of Joint), and *Twelfth Night* (National Theatre). www.theasifkhan.com

Nona Shepphard – Director

Nona Shepphard is a freelance writer and director, with over a hundred and fifty productions and forty commissioned plays to her credit. She is Associate Director of the Royal Academy of Dramatic Art, and International Consultant at the Lir Academy in Dublin. She wrote the adaptation, book and lyrics for *Therese Raquin* which transferred from the Finborough Theatre to the Park Theatre London in 2015 and *Draupadi, Princess of Fire* for The Sujata Banerjee Dance Company last spring. She spent Autumn 2016 in Manila where she created and directed *The Tempest Re-Imagined* at PETA Theatre; this was a fusion of Shakespeare's play with survivors' stories from the catastrophic hurricane Haiyan in 2013. She has recently returned from San Antonio,Texas, where she directed *A Midsummer Night's Dream.*

Mila Sanders – Designer

Mila trained at the University of Wales, Aberystwyth and Wimbledon School of Art.

Her designs include: *Love, Bombs and Apples* (Arcola), *The Wind in the Willows* (Birmingham Old Rep), *Darknet* (Southwark Playhouse), *Soapbox* (Talawa), *Queen of the Nile* (Hull Truck), *Dogs Barking* (RADA), *Parallax*, T*he Door Never Closes*, *All the Little Things We Crushed* (Almeida),

The Only Way is Chelsea's (York Theatre Royal), *The Rite of Spring / Romeo and Juliet* (Concert Theatre), *Snakes and Ladders* (Rolemop), *Jelly Bean Jack* (Little Angel), *Pub Quiz* (New Writing North), *A Midsummer Night's Dream* (NT Education).

As Costume Designer: *Macbeth, Twelfth Night* (NT Discover), *The Little Mermaid, Pinocchio* (Kazzum), *Tombstone Tales and Boothill Ballads* (Arcola), *Jason and the Argonauts* (BAC, Warwick Arts Centre and tour), *St George and the Dragon* (Warwick Arts Centre) and *Unfolding Andersen* (Theatre-rites).

Andy Grange – Lighting Designer

Andy's work includes: *Little Red Riding Hood, Hansel & Gretel* (Hertford Theatre, Hertford), *The Collector* (KB Productions, UK Tour / Greenwich Theatre), *Hysteria, The Birthday Party, Waiting For Godot, Absent Friends, Entertaining Mr. Sloane, Betrayal, The Importance of Being Earnest* (London Classic Theatre, UK / Ireland Tour), T*ess of the d'Urbervilles, Robinson Crusoe, Animus, Sunshine on Leith, Beauty & The Beast, Welcome to Thebes, Just So, Aladdin, Electra* (The MTA, London), *Romeo & Juliet, Pride & Prejudice, Bottom's Dream, Arabian Nights, Richard III, The Merchant of Venice, The Canterbury Tales, Much Ado About Nothing, Hamlet* (Queen Mary 2, Royal Court Theatre), *Crimes in Hot Countries, Man & Superman, Woyzeck, The Shape of Things, Motortown, Titus Andronicus* (RADA), *And In The End* (Jermyn Street Theatre), *An Intimate Evening with Ruthie Henshall* (re-lighter) (National Tour), and *Mansfield Park* (re-lighter) (Theatre Royal Bury St. Edmunds, National tour).

Other work includes lighting design for Psycho Nacirema (James Franco, PACE Gallery, London). Andy also works regularly for RADA Enterprises and Tara Theatre.

www.andygrange.com

James Hesford – Composer & Sound Designer

James Hesford is an award-winning musician / composer working in theatre, film and television and he regularly receives commissions for chamber works. Credits include: BBC, Channel 5, Channel 4, BBC World News, Lyric Hammersmith, BAC, Little Angel Theatre, Polka Theatre, West Yorkshire, Playhouse etc. Fidelio Trio, Bekova Trio, Sonore Trio, Mardi Brass. He recently scored the feature film *Finding Fatimah* – ICON – which will be on general release in April 2017 and the documentary *Twilight of the Master* – score James Hesford – has now been nominated for the Best Short Documentary by the Festival Du Cinéma Européen.

CAST

Beruce Khan – Shaz

Beruce Khan trained at RADA.

Theatre credits include: *Gary Tank Commander: Mission Quite Possible* (SSE Hydro Arena), *Henry V* (Regent's Park Open Air Theatre), *Hamlet* (Shakespeare's Globe International Tour), *Romeo & Juliet* (Shakespeare's Globe), *Henry V* (Shakespeare's Globe), *The Madness of George III* (Apollo Theatre), *History Boys* (Theatre Royal Bath), *The Black Album* (Tara Arts & National Theatre co-production).

Rez Kempton – Ali

Rez trained at Rose Bruford College.

Theatre includes: *Little Revolution* (Almeida), *Khandan* (Royal Court), *Drawing The Line* (Hampstead), *Gandhi and Coconuts* (Arcola), *The Hot Zone* (Lyric), *The Fortune Club* (Tricycle), *The Battle of Green Lanes* (Theatre Royal Stratford East), *Hirja* (West Yorkshire Playhouse), *Nativity* (Birmingham Rep) and *The Arbor* (Crucible)

Film includes: *The Mummy*, *Amar Akbar & Tony*, *Life Goes On*, *Reuniting the Rubins*, *I Can't Think Straight*, *Mystic Masseur*, *My Son of the Fanatic* and *Brothers in Trouble*.

Television includes: *Adha Cup*, *Spooks*, *Lee Evans: So What Now?*, *Desperados*, *Roger Roger*, *Bash*, *Banged Up Abroad*, *Doctors* and *Trial by Jury*.

Mitesh Soni – Faisal

Mitesh trained at the Guildford School of Acting.

Theatre credits include: *Home Truths* (Bunker Theatre / Cardboard Citz), *Rudolf* (West Yorkshire Playhouse), *Paradise of The Assassins* (Tara Arts), *Coming Up* (Watford Palace), *Macbeth* (Tara Arts – UK Tour), *Romeo & Juliet* (National Theatre), *The Good Person of Sichuan* (Colchester), *Arabian Nights* (Manchester Library Theatre), *This Place Means* (Greenwich), *The Firework Maker's Daughter* (Theatre by the Lake, Keswick), *The Rise & Fall of Little Voice* (Dukes, Lancaster), *Peter Pan* (New Vic Stoke), *Rafta Rafta* (Bolton Octagon / New Vic Stoke), *The Jungle Book* (Birmingham Stage Company UK Tour), *Cloud Pictures* (Polka Theatre), *Mercury Fur* (Goldsmiths), *Lord of the Flies* (Pilot Theatre UK tour), *Meteorite* (Hampstead Theatre), *Cloud 9* (Queen Mother Theatre) and *Blood Wedding* (Edinburgh Festival).

Film credits include: *Rise of The Footsoldier 2*, *Syriana*, *Ghost of Life*, *Nine Lives London*, *Alpha Mayall* and *Lost Night*.

Television credits include: *The Agency*, *Run*, *Threesome* and *The Canterbury Tales*.

Awards: 2012 Manchester Theatre Award – Best Ensemble – *Arabian Nights*

Shireen Farkhoy – Samina

Shireen trained at Bristol Old Vic Theatre School. Theatre credits include: *Haste Ye Back* (Arcola Theatre), *The Collector* (London Classic Theatre), *The Bare Project* (Sheffield

Theatres), *Sam Wanamaker Festival* (Shakespeare's Globe), *The Heresy of Love* (Bristol Old Vic), *The Grand Gesture* (Tobacco Factory), *Crap Dad* (West Yorkshire Playhouse), *After Sunset* (Opera North), *Hansel and Gretel* (Wakefield Theatre Royal) and *The Genie of Samarkand* (Tara Arts). TV credits include: *The 'A' Word* (BBC), *Waterloo Road* (BBC) and *The Royal Today* (ITV)

Nigel Hastings – Andy

Theatre includes: *And Then Come The Nightjars* (Theatre 503), *What Falls Apart* (Live Newcastle), *Henry VI*, *Othello* (Shakespeare's Globe), *Journey's End* (Duke of York's), *Gone* (New Ambassadors), *Kindertransport* (Vaudeville Theatre), *Hitchcock Blonde* (Hull Truck), *Animal Farm*, *The Lady In The Van* (West Yorkshire Playhouse), *Amadeus* (Crucible Theatre), *Pravda* (Chichester / Birmingham), *Jerusalem Syndrome* (Soho Theatre), *All My Sons* (Theatre Royal, Plymouth), *Twelfth Night* (Edinburgh Lyceum), *The Devils* (Theatr Clwyd), *As You Like It*, *A Midsummer Night's Dream* (Regent's Park Open Air Theatre) and *Pride and Prejudice* (Royal Exchange, Manchester).

Television and Film includes: *Peaky Blinders*, *The Shadow Line*, *Hustle*, *The Commander*, *A Touch Of Frost*, *Eastenders*, *The Ring*, *Cadfael*, *Soldier Soldier*, *A Bit Of A Do*, *Four Weddings and a Funeral*, *Hostage* and *The Unbeatables*.

Production Credits

Written by Asif Khan

Produced by AIK Productions and Tara Arts

The production is generously supported by The Carne Trust and Arts Council England.

Cast

Beruce Khan	SHAZ
Rez Kempton	ALI
Mitesh Soni	FAISAL
Shireen Farkhoy	SAMINA
Nigel Hastings	ANDY

Creative & Production

Nona Shepphard	Director
Mila Sanders	Designer
James Hesford	Composer & Sound Design
Andy Grange	Lighting Design
Shaz McGee	Production Manager
Emily Moitoi-Sturman	Company Stage Manager
Sophie Stoddart	Deputy Stage Manager
Gemma Martin	Rehearsal Assistant Stage Manager
Hilary Lewis	Costume Supervisor
Renny Krupinski	Fight Director
Michaela Kennen	Voice Coach
Elin Morgan	Press Agent at Mobius PR
Alan Bowyer	Trailer
Basement 94	Set Construction

UK National Tour May – July 2017

Tara Theatre
Wed 17 to Sat 27 May, 7.30pm & 3pm Sat matinee
plus 2.30pm matinee Thurs 25 May
Box Office: 020 8333 4457
www.tara-arts.com

Arcola Theatre
Tues 30 May & Sat 24 June 8pm
Box Office: 020 7503 1645
www.arcolatheatre.com

Norwich Arts Centre
Tues 27 June, 8pm
Box Office: 01603 660 352
www.norwichartscentre.co.uk

Rada Festival, Gielgud Theatre
Thurs 29 & Fri 30 June, Thurs 7pm & Fri 2pm
Box Office: 020 7636 7076
www.rada.ac.uk

Theatre Royal Margate
Sun 2 July, 7.30pm
Box Office: 01843 292 795
www.theatreroyalmargate.com

Queen's Hall Arts
Tues 4 July, 7.30pm
Box Office: 01434 652477
www.queenshall.co.uk

The Customs House
Thurs 6 July, 7.30pm
Box Office: 0191 454 1234
www.customshouse.co.uk

Bradford Literature Festival
Fri 7 July, 7.30pm
Box Office: 01274 233 185
www.bradfordlitfest.co.uk

See also: www.blacktheatrelive.co.uk

COMBUSTION

'An Arab has no superiority over a non-Arab, nor does a non-Arab have any superiority over an Arab; a white has no superiority over a black, nor does a black have any superiority over a white; [none have superiority over another] except by piety and good action.'

– Prophet Muhammad (PBUH)

Combustion was first performed on Wednesday 17th May 2107 at Tara Theatre London.

Setting

Bradford, Frizinghall. 2017. Summer.

Characters

Shaz, 30	Owner of a car mechanics garage. Alpha male, protective, the boss.
Ali, 30	Friend of Shaz. Joker, loose cannon, loud.
Faisal, 30	Friend of Shaz. Simple, friendly, skilled mechanic.
Samina, 20	Sister of Shaz. Peace Studies student at Bradford University, proudly wears the hijab, sharp.
Andy, 50	Father, member of English Defence, lonely.

Notes

All characters speak with a Bradford accent.

'/' signals an interruption.

SCENE 1

Shazad's Mechanics Garage. 6th August. Sunset. Possibly the final night of Ramadan. Shaz and Ali at work. Shaz checks his phone.

SHAZ   It's time.

ALI   Iftari?

SHAZ   Yeah.

ALI   Fucking yes!

SHAZ   Oi... you're not supposed to swear during this time/

ALI   Is Faisal not back?

SHAZ   Nope.

ALI   Where the fuck is he?! It's only round the corner!

SHAZ   Sabhar [patience] OK? Here, I've got some kajoor [dates].

Shaz plays the Azaan [call to prayer] from his phone. They say the prayer to break fast, and eat the dates. Also water. Silence.

ALI   Tastes like magic.

Faisal comes in with a plastic carrier containing three takeaways.

ALI   What the hell were you doing all this time?!

FAISAL   Soz bro, there was a humongous queue 'n that. Everybody breaking their fast innit.

Ali grabs the bag.

ALI   You got ma chicken wrap as well?

FAISAL   Yeah.

SHAZ   Sit down Fes... have a kajoor.

Faisal breaks his fast with a date. Ali takes his food out and starts eating. Shaz takes out his own and Faisal's.

ALI   So what's happening on the rishta [marriage] front?

Beat.

SHAZ   Nothing.

ALI   Don't talk shit. I heard you and your mum in the kitchen.

Beat.

SHAZ   I've got summat on the go, but I'm not talking about it.

ALI   What? Why?

SHAZ   Nazzir [evil eye].

ALI   Shut up Nazzir! You can tell me, I'm like your brother.

FAISAL   Yeah tell us bro.

Beat.

SHAZ   Uncle Akram knows a good family who have a daughter looking for rishta, so mum's set summat up for tomorrow.

ALI   What's her name? What she do?

SHAZ   Naila. Pharmacist.

FAISAL   Nice!

SHAZ   Wears the hijab 'n that.

ALI   MashAllah! You got a photo?

SHAZ   Yeah.

ALI   Show us.

SHAZ   Nope.

FAISAL   Does she have any sisters?

SHAZ   Why?

FAISAL	Could do with a hand bro.
ALI	Faisal's desperate man.
SHAZ	Your mum still got you on that site?
FAISAL	Yeah bro. I've gotta good profile on it 'n that. It's just...
SHAZ	What?
FAISAL	Once they see ma photo they stop responding.
ALI	What photo you using?
FAISAL	This one. *(Faisal pulls out his phone to show his photo)*
ALI	That's fucking horrible man! Take another. And don't smile on it.
SHAZ	Show me Fes.

Faisal shows Shaz.

SHAZ	It's alright. I'd say wear a shirt instead. Makes you look successful. And take the shot outside. Better light.
ALI	Bad advice with his face.
SHAZ	Don't be a twat Ali.
FAISAL	It's OK Shaz... he's just fooling around 'n that.
ALI	Course I am.
FAISAL	But seriously... if your mum knows of any nice girls then tell me. I don't mind if she's a bit fat.
ALI	You're *really* desperate aren't ya?
FAISAL	Some of the nicer girls are a bit bigger.
ALI	They don't have to have a muffin top to be nice Fes.
FAISAL	Muffin what?

ALI	You've seen those birds where all the cherbi [fat] is drooping over the jeans... looks like a muffin.
SHAZ	Like that Laura you went out with?
ALI	That was yonks ago man.
FAISAL	He's got his hopes on Samina now.
SHAZ	He touches Samina he's dead.
ALI	I wouldn't do that man. You'll turn into Tony Montana and shoot me.
FAISAL	He said he's got five more years of freedom before he gives his mum the green light.
SHAZ	All men want to play around Ali, but it's not Islamic.
FAISAL	Qur'an says you complete half ya religion when you get married 'n that.
SHAZ	That's right.
ALI	So what about the second half? Get married again?

The boys laugh.

FAISAL	Nice one bro, nice one!
ALI	Five more years and then ma mum can go on the search in Pakistan.
SHAZ	What's wrong with Bradford girls?
ALI	No traditions.
SHAZ	Naila's very traditional.
ALI	You haven't met her yet.
SHAZ	I've been phoning her everyday for two months.
FAISAL	Really?
ALI	Some of these birds can't even knock up a roti... fucking shocking.

FAISAL	Yeah that is pretty shocking.
SHAZ	Naila can.
ALI	They just talk too much. Never shut up.
FAISAL	Yeah they do talk a lot.
ALI	Then again, they won't be talking when I've got ma cock in their mouth.

Faisal and Ali find this hilarious. Shaz smiles and shakes his head.

SHAZ	Tauba, tauba [God forbid, God forbid]. We're still in Ramzaan you know.
ALI	Last night bro. It's Eid tomorrow!
SHAZ	Has it been confirmed?
ALI	Bloody hope so man. Rosay [fasting] are killing me.
FAISAL	Ma dad said he's gonna do Eid tomorrow coz he's got a day off.
SHAZ	Nah that's not right. Can't choose shit like that.
ALI	If someone's seen the moon, that's it. Everybody should do it.
FAISAL	I'll have to do it tomorrow if ma dad does it.
SHAZ	InshAllah, we'll find out at the Masjid later. They get the moon sighting from Saudi.
ALI	Telling you man these rosay... ma arms have gone all skinny.
FAISAL	I found 'em pretty easy.
SHAZ	It's coz you don't wake up for Sehri [breakfast before fasting].
ALI	Can't get up man. I tried.

SHAZ	Missing your namaaz [prayer] in the morning as well... no point fasting all day if you don't pray/
ALI	No lectures daddy.
SHAZ	Praying is the most important thing.
ALI	Yeah I know that Shaz.
SHAZ	Fine.
ALI	If it's Eid tomorrow let's go check out that new snooker joint in town.
FAISAL	It's not open coz English Defence are coming.
ALI *(shocked)*	What?!
SHAZ	You not heard? Been all over the news.
ALI	Fuck no. Din't know this!
FAISAL	They were telling us at mosque.
ALI	On Eid?! Mother fuckers!
SHAZ	Best thing to do is ignore them completely.
ALI	Why the fuck are they allowed to come here?
SHAZ	Coz of those cunts at 'Imran's Motors' innit. Grooming that... what's her name... Girl P.
FAISAL	Girl T.
SHAZ	Girl T. They're doing a protest about that.
FAISAL	It's just a protection name 'n that.
ALI	So what have the rest of Bradford got to do with it? They've been arrested.
SHAZ	They blame Islam for it. Think the Muslim community should stand up and take responsibility.
ALI	Dicks. When some gorah [white man] does summat wrong we don't blame everyone

with a white face do we? ... Din't those two white men groom a load of 13 year old boys recently/

FAISAL   Yeah ma dad was telling me about that/

ALI   Using social media sites. One of 'em was HIV infected. Nobody seems to be saying the 'white community' should stand up and take responsibility for it are they? The fucking media man. The media are the biggest tool of the government... the biggest propaganda tool you can ever get.

FAISAL   Ma dad said he's only gonna watch Al Jazeera now.

ALI   How long them cunts go down for?

SHAZ   Thirty years.

ALI   Fuuuck.

SHAZ   There were three of 'em. Mum was telling me. One of her friends knows someone from their family. The uncle... the older one... he's run off back to Pakistan.

ALI   Not gonna find him now. Prob'ly hiding in the Himalayas somewhere.

SHAZ   Dickheads. I mean... they had a good business... respectable family... throw it all away. They've got a sister who's about twenty-five wanting to get married... good luck with that.

ALI   Faisal'll marry her.

FAISAL *(interested)* What's she look like?

SHAZ   That family has now been fucked. That little girl...

FAISAL   Girl T.

SHAZ	Her life's done. She'll never recover. This is the kind of shameful shit that wrecks our image. Course English Defence are gonna jump on it.
ALI	Yeah but coming on Eid! I'll go Jihad on them... bomb all the racist cunts.
SHAZ	You see that's exactly the type of shit that's making us all look bad.
ALI	What shit?
SHAZ	The shit you just said.
ALI	I'm only kidding you twat.
SHAZ	That's why everyone hates us these days. They want us to react to it. Get angry, bomb summat.
ALI	Why shouldn't we get angry, when they're on the streets shouting 'Allah Allah who the F is Allah'? If I hear any of that shit tomorrow they'll be sorry they ever came to Bradford... they're coming into the lion's den here in Bradford I'm telling ya. We're fucking Ottomans here man.
SHAZ	So what shall we do? Riot again?
ALI	At least we're not pussies. Least we stick up for ourselves.
SHAZ	By stabbing soldiers in the street?
ALI	Shut up/
SHAZ	What are we doing to make ourselves look decent? If some guy decides to burn the Qur'an in America, why do our lot have to cause a big riot about it. Islam's bigger than that man. Burning one copy of the Qur'an isn't gonna destroy Islam. And that stupid shit you just said... 'Go Jihad on 'em and

bomb 'em' ... that's exactly what they think of us. You're feeding right into the hands of Tommy Powell there... he's never going to change his views about us lot if you say stupid shit like that.

ALI   You really think I care what *he* thinks?

SHAZ   She was fucking *twelve*. Raped by 'em all. Burnt with cigarettes. Had initials of one of 'em burnt into her. Made pregnant and forced to take some back street abortion shit. Imagine if that happened to one of *our* sisters.

ALI   If it was one of our girls there'd never be this much press about it.

SHAZ   Abused by a string of customers who paid to have a piece of her.

ALI   They were prob'ly told she was older than twelve.

SHAZ   I'm sick of feeling like I have to convince non-Muslims that I'm not a terrorist/

ALI   Bet she looks older than twelve/

SHAZ   Not a fucking groomer/

ALI   Girls always look older these days/

SHAZ   Why should I have to do that?

ALI   Why you getting caught up with what non-Muslims think?

SHAZ   Since that Girl P story/

FAISAL   Girl T.

SHAZ   Hit the news... I've been worried someone's gonna see ma mum or Samina in a hijab and revenge attack on 'em. Why should I have to feel like that?

ALI	That old Muslim man got stabbed in Heaton outside the Masjid by some white lads... where was the coverage on that?
SHAZ	You're not listening to me/
ALI	I am listening to you... I'm worried about Ami as well. She wants to go for her daily walk... I don't let her.
SHAZ	Exactly.
FAISAL	I go with ma mum to the shops to shield her 'n that.
ALI	Prob'ly be the other way round with you Fes. She'd have to protect you.
SHAZ	Seeing no white customers anymore. Business suffering coz o' this shit. Stay out of their way... ignore 'em... don't give 'em any attention... don't give 'em any press.
FAISAL	Or give 'em tea.
ALI	What?
FAISAL	Give 'em tea like that mosque did in Blackburn. Tea 'n biscuits.
SHAZ	That's Islam! English Defence tried to cause a riot outside that mosque. The mosque played it right. Gave 'em tea and biscuits... said let's chat. Calmed things right down. No need for anger.
ALI	If someone draws an offensive cartoon of the Prophet are you not angry?
SHAZ	I'm fuming.
ALI	Are *you* angry by that Fes?
FAISAL	Yeah.
ALI	There you go.

SHAZ	But that doesn't mean go out and kill people.
ALI	Shouldn't draw offensive cartoons then should they? They want freedom of speech, we'll have the freedom to react. They slap us and then tell us how to react to being slapped.
SHAZ	Feed right into their hands.
ALI	OK bro, so let's go into town with a tray full of tea and biscuits... and cupcakes... like pussies... maybe suck their cocks while we're at it/
SHAZ	Dickhead.
ALI	Give 'em a smack... knock 'em out... that'll calm things right down... trust me.

Samina enters with a Tupperware box, and some chapattis wrapped in foil.

ALI	Sometimes when you punch back it warns people... shows 'em that we won't take any shit... scares 'em... makes 'em fear us. Then they won't say shit.
SHAZ	Shut the fuck up and eat.
SAMINA	What you talking about?
SHAZ	Nothing.
SAMINA	Ami told me to drop these off.
SHAZ	We got a takeaway instead.
SAMINA	Have this as well.
SHAZ	Nah stuffed already man.
SAMINA	Ali and Faisal will have it.
ALI	I'm good Sammy. Ramzaan's made ma stomach shrink.

FAISAL   I'll have some.

ALI   Fat fuck.

SHAZ   Giz it here, I'll warm it up.

Shaz goes out to microwave.

ALI   Look good Sammy.

SAMINA *(playful)* Shut up Ali.

ALI   Serious. Looking trim. In't she Fes?

FAISAL   Yeah.

SAMINA   You can stop it coz it's Ramzaan.

ALI   Might be Eid tomorrow. Here... Eid present. *(Pulls out some money)* Buy a nice outfit 'n that.

Samina doesn't accept.

ALI   Go on take it.

SAMINA   You don't have money to give Ali.

ALI   Rude not to accept.

SAMINA   Fine. *(She takes it)* Don't think yer in there though.

ALI   Ya tight.

SAMINA   No offence, but I'm only marrying a doctor.

ALI   What's wrong with a car mechanic? Your brother's a mechanic.

SAMINA   It's his own business at least.

ALI   What if I became a doctor, would you marry me then?

SAMINA   I'd think about it.

ALI   Fucking hell... I'm getting somewhere.

SAMINA   Faisal's got more chance than you.

FAISAL *(smiling)* Have I?

ALI *(to Faisal)* Don't be thick, she's using you to insult me.

SAMINA   At least Faisal's a gent.

ALI   You're not Faisal's type... he likes fat girls. Anyway, I can be a gent. I can be whatever you want. You want me to be a doctor? Right! I'm gonna apply to do medicine tomorrow... how fucking romantic is that?

SAMINA *(playful)* Such an idiot. If Shaz caught you chatting to me like this he'd break your legs.

ALI   Shaz doesn't need to know our secrets. It's just between me and you.

FAISAL   Actually me too coz I'm here as well.

ALI   Faisal won't say owt... he's ma main man... ain't ya Fes?

FAISAL   Yeah.

ALI   Hey did *you* know English Defence are coming tomorrow?

SAMINA   Course. I'm going down there to make a speech at the counter demo.

ALI   Really?

SAMINA   You coming?

Shaz returns.

SHAZ   There you go Faisal.

FAISAL   Nice one.

ALI   Hear this bro?

SAMINA   Ali *(signalling not to mention)*.

SHAZ   What?

SAMINA   Nothing.

SHAZ   What's up?

SAMINA	I'm just doing a thing with 'Bradford For Peace'.
SHAZ	What thing?
SAMINA	A counter demo.
SHAZ	Tomorrow?
SAMINA	Yeah.
SHAZ	Over my dead body you are.
SAMINA	What?
SHAZ	I said no, you're not going.
SAMINA	It's all planned bhai. I'm making a speech.
SHAZ	You'll be doing no such thing.
SAMINA	We'll see about that *(goes to exit)*.
SHAZ *(firm)*	Oi! Come here! I said you're not fucking going. I mean it. Nobody here is fucking going. You get me?

Beat.

SHAZ	It might be Eid tomorrow. You'll be staying indoors. Help mum out. Play with your make-up.

Beat.

SHAZ	Now go on. Get inside.

Samina goes to exit.

SHAZ	Tell Ami I'm going to Thravia [Ramadan prayers] tonight... I'll be in in two minutes.
SAMINA	Right.

Samina exits.

ALI	Bit harsh there bro.
SHAZ	You boys coming?
FAISAL	Yeah... last night innit.

SHAZ	Ali?
ALI	Suppose. Get a lecture otherwise. Which Masjid you going to?
SHAZ	Howard Street.
ALI	Right, I'll join you. We'll have to finish off that dude's Beemer tomorrow.
SHAZ	No-can-do. Gotta do it tonight. He's coming to pick it up first thing.
ALI	Fucking hell.
SHAZ	Your fault being on your phone all day.
ALI	Faisal do us a favour would you?
SHAZ	Don't get Faisal to do it. He's worked his arse off. Finish the job off, we'll see you at the Masjid.
ALI	At least give us a hand.
SHAZ	Faisal's taught you how to do it. Make sure it's done.
ALI	Right boss.
SHAZ	Switch all lights off and lock up before you leave. Faisal come on.
FAISAL	I haven't finished eating bro.
SHAZ	Yeah I know, but I ain't having this guy persuade you to do his job after I leave. You can eat at mine.

Faisal gathers his things.

FAISAL	See you in a bit bro.

They leave. Ali is left on his own. After a few seconds he checks his phone. Three missed calls.

ALI	Fuck's sake.

He dials the number.

ALI   Listen you dumb fuck. Don't ring me again!
                 I told you. Delete my fucking number!

He hangs up.

SCENE 2

Shazad's Garage. Following day. 7th August. Morning.
It's Eid, after the prayer. Shaz has just dealt with the
customer who collected the BMW Ali repaired. He's in
his Eid prayer outfit, sorting out the paperwork. Ali and
Faisal enter.

ALI   Eid Mubarak bro!

SHAZ   Eid Mubarak man!

They all embrace in the traditional manner – three hugs
followed by a handshake.

SHAZ   Eid Mubarak Fes.

FAISAL   Eid Mubarak bro!

ALI   Checking up on me?

SHAZ   You did a good job. For once. Dude was
                   happy with it.

ALI   Fucking hell... someone's happy with me at
                   least.

SHAZ   What you mean?

ALI   Another yelling match with dad. Great
                   start to Eid. Anyway forget that... check
                   this! *(He pulls out a newspaper)* That sala
                   kutha leader Tommy Powell quits English
                   Defence!

SHAZ   What? Really?! *(Shaz grabs the paper and*
                   reads)

ALI	Yeah! Finally realized he's got no chance against Islam. Thakbir!
FAISAL	Allah-hu Akbar!
ALI	Thakbir!
FAISAL	Allah-hu Akbar! *(Ali and Faisal laugh and celebrate)*
SHAZ	Guys... fucking hell... let me read.

He reads.

SHAZ	Wow.
ALI	Gave up, coz Islam can't be broken. Islam wins bro! Thakbir!
FAISAL	Allah-hu Akbar!
SHAZ	Fuck's sake guys.
ALI	It's celebration time man!
SHAZ	Wonder what's gonna happen with the demo today then?
FAISAL	Ma dad said it's still going ahead 'n that.
SHAZ	That'll be interesting.
ALI	Lets pop into town and check it out. I need to pick up some mithai [Asian sweets] anyway.
SHAZ	No way.
ALI	Just take a look man. It'll be hilarious seeing all them English Defence fucks abandoned by their leader.
SHAZ *(firm)*	We've been fasting for twenty-nine fucking days. It's Eid. We're gonna celebrate and enjoy ourselves. Besides I'm off to meet Naila.
ALI	Oh yeah.

SHAZ	And I know what you're like, you'll get yourself arrested again. You wanna get yourself banged up again? *(Firm)* You go down there I'll be pissed.
ALI	Got another dad here Fes.
SHAZ	Can see the headlines already, 'Pakistani man from Shazad's Garage/
ALI	Alright Shaz... bloody hell.
SHAZ	You think they'll come up our way?
ALI	If they do, you take the wrench, I'll take the tyre pump?
SHAZ	Tyre pump?
ALI	Stick it up their arse and pump the racism out of 'em.
FAISAL	What about me?
ALI	You're best staying out of the way... you could get hurt.
SHAZ	Well it's a good job we're closed today.
ALI	What time ya going to see that chick?
SHAZ	Now. Just waiting for Ami to get ready. Her dad wants to chat to me on his own first.
ALI	Can't give you any advice on that I'm afraid. *My* dad can't bear to look at me.
FAISAL	You'll be OK bro, dads love you 'n that.
ALI	My old man would easily trade me in for you. Good Muslim, runs his own business.
FAISAL	MashAllah.
SHAZ	Yeah, well it was either start my own business or work full time in restaurants, doing dead end jobs like washing up dishes, shampoo factories. Struck me, do I carry on doing this for the rest of ma life, or

do I actually make something of it? I was
hungry for success. I wanted to prove to
all the people... who always put me down...
thought negative about me... and about
Bradford... that... you know... that I can do
this.

ALI   You see that's the type of shit you need to
say to her dad... he'll be well impressed.
And then slip in that you pray five times a
day.

SHAZ   It's worked out perfectly for me here.
People don't think it's possible to make it in
Bradford, but there's lots of examples, me
being one of 'em. Early days yet, but sky's
the limit.

FAISAL *(amazed)* You inspire me bro.

SHAZ   If you wanna do summat you've just gotta
dedicate yourself to it one hundred percent
and never give up/

ALI   OK bro. Save this for her dad.

FAISAL   Let him finish 'n that!

SHAZ   You've just got to stay positive and really,
really want it. I mean look at me... started
fixing cars in ma back yard... d'int have
many customers... but made sure every
single customer was happy... built up ma
reputation... now look... got my own car
garage... right next door to my family.

ALI   Never pay this guy a compliment again Fes.
Just get motivational speeches in return.

SHAZ   Next year I've got plans to expand this place
inshAllah. Have a separate section over
there for modifying... pimping up cars...
blinging 'em... potential in that area... huge.

ALI	That's a bloody good idea actually/
SHAZ	You gotta know who your market is bro... here in Bradford that's what our lot are into... but not just thinking Bradford... I've got plans to go global... design my own gear... bumpers... spoilers... stuff like that... if you've got a website... can sell all over the world. America, China, Japan.
FAISAL	You should be a judge on Dragon's Den bro.
ALI	Stop sucking his cock Fes.

Samina enters. She's wearing an outfit, with hints of lime green on it.

SAMINA	Ami's waiting for you.
SHAZ	Shit better go.
SAMINA	Looking nice bhai.
SHAZ	Have to make 'n effort.
SAMINA *(checking him)*	You got some Issey Miyake on?
SHAZ	Loads. Don't forget to lock up.
ALI	I won't.
SHAZ	And switch the lights off.
ALI	Don't worry bro! Everything's in safe hands. Go charm that kuri [girl].
SAMINA	Good luck bhai.

Shaz leaves.

ALI	Am I gonna get an Eid Mubarak kiss?
SAMINA	No.
ALI	Have to say, that outfit compliments your figure nicely. In't that right Fes?
FAISAL	Yeah.
ALI	Nice 'n tight.

SAMINA *(playful)* Shut up Ali.

ALI   Nice colour as well. MashAllah. Suits ya.

SAMINA   They're 'BFP' colours.

ALI   BF what?

SAMINA   Bradford For Peace.

ALI *(beat; then Ali realises)* Oh no Sammy. Shaz ain't gonna like this.

SAMINA   Shaz isn't here. And thanks for dropping me in it last night.

ALI   Well in the words of Shazad Iqbal, 'You're not fucking going'.

SAMINA *(sarcastic)* Ha. Ha.

ALI   I'm serious Sammy.

SAMINA   Oh you're serious are you?

ALI   Your bro will fucking murder you. And me, if I don't stop you.

SAMINA   Don't need permission off my brother thank you very much.

ALI   Don't give me any of that girl power shit Sammy. You think I don't wanna go into town myself?

SAMINA   Well come on then. Let's go.

ALI   Your brother's right. It's Eid, we should be celebrating. Tell her Fes.

FAISAL   What shall a' say?

SAMINA   Why have you turned into a good little boy?

ALI   Hundreds of English Defence thugs are gonna be there.

SAMINA   We're doing a peaceful demo Ali.

ALI   It's not safe for Muslims.

SAMINA   I'm a big girl.

ALI   Sorry Sammy.

Ali closes the door and blocks her path.

SAMINA   Ali come on. Stop being stupid.

ALI   You're gonna stay here and celebrate Eid like a good Muslim girl. Hold her down Fes.

FAISAL *(scared)* What?

Samina tries to exit. Ali blocks her path.

SAMINA   Fuck's sake Ali! What is wrong with you?!

ALI   You shouldn't have told me Sammy. Big mistake.

SAMINA   You're really pissing me off now. I'm making a speech. Get out of my way!

ALI   Hold her back Fes.

FAISAL   What?

SAMINA   Ali. Get the fuck out of my way. Now.

ALI   Faisal.

SAMINA   Don't even fucking try it Fes!

ALI   Shaz will kill me Sammy. Have to look out for myself.

SAMINA   Move!

ALI   Try 'n leave... I'm just gonna hold onto your leg.

Beat.

SAMINA   Fine.

ALI   You're gonna stay?

SAMINA   Yes.

ALI   You're not gonna go?

SAMINA   Yes!

ALI   Bloody hell Fes. The girl listened to someone for once.

SAMINA	Right then. Since we're celebrating... let's have fun.
ALI	That's more like it.
SAMINA	Yeah, let's have some fun.
ALI	The back seat of that car's comfy. Leave us to it Fes.
FAISAL	Where shall I go?
SAMINA	Let me try some make-up on you.
ALI	What?
SAMINA	Bit of eye shadow/
ALI	Fuck off
SAMINA	Mascara, lippy/
ALI	Fuck off!

Faisal finds this funny.

SAMINA	Come on, just for a bit of fun.
ALI	Why does it have to be girly fun?
SAMINA	It's Eid.
ALI	Do it on Faisal.
SAMINA	You've got longer lashes.

Ali doesn't respond.

SAMINA	If you're gonna stop me going to this demo, then I'm gonna have some fun.

Beat.

SAMINA	You'll enjoy it.

Beat.

ALI	Fine. If it means you stay here. Fine.

Faisal laughs.

ALI	Shut it Faisal.
SAMINA	Right, lie back on this chair.

Samina gets some make-up products out of her bag. Ali lies back onto the chair.

ALI Quite a collection you got there.

SAMINA Right, we'll start with a bit of foundation... and then move onto your eyes.

Samina starts applying the make-up.

FAISAL I'm recording this. *(Pulls out his phone camera)*

ALI Faisal put that shit away.

SAMINA Stop moving, Ali.

ALI Faisal, I mean it.

SAMINA Let him have fun, you can delete it afterwards. Anyway you'll be able to watch back the transformation.

ALI *(to Faisal)* Cheeky twat.

SAMINA You've got good skin actually.

ALI Have I?

SAMINA Yeah.

ALI You should run your own make-up business 'n that.

SAMINA I wouldn't mind that.

ALI Specialize in bridal work. Lots of money to be made.

SAMINA Really?

ALI Every Tom, Dick and Muhammed getting married these days.

SAMINA You're right.

ALI This is alright actually. Quite relaxing 'n that.

SAMINA Told you you'll enjoy it.

ALI	You feeling any attraction towards me being this close?
SAMINA	No, I'm not.
ALI	Feeling the heat?
SAMINA	Just keep still, will you?
ALI	Can't help it. An attractive girl being this close to me. You smell good... what perfume is it?
SAMINA	Ghost.
ALI	Smells good.

Faisal comes closer with the camera.

ALI	Faisal, you're really starting to piss me off now.
SAMINA	Relax, Ali. Unless you want me to poke you in the eye.
ALI	So do you know much about this Naila?
SAMINA	Seen her photo. She'll have to be summat special if she wants to marry ma bro.
ALI	Getting all protective are ya?
SAMINA	Only got one bro. If she's not right for him, then I'll say.
ALI *(teasing)*	Seeing a bit of jealousy there, Sammy.
SAMINA	What have I got to be jealous about?
ALI	Samina's getting jealous, Samina's getting jealous/
SAMINA	I *am* gonna poke you in the eye you know.
ALI	Hey have you got any fat friends who might like Faisal?
SAMINA	Fat?
ALI	Like Pavarotti fat.
SAMINA	Why fat?

ALI	Faisal likes 'em fat.
SAMINA	Really?
ALI	Bigger the better.
FAISAL	No I said I don't mind if they're a bit bigger. Normally those girls get ignored, but some of 'em have good personalities 'n that.
SAMINA	What type of personality you after, Faisal?
FAISAL	You know... be good to ma parents... be a good Muslim 'n that. I like girls who laugh a lot.
ALI	You're in luck there Faisal, coz every girl will laugh at you.
SAMINA	Don't be cruel. At least he's not judging girls on their looks. He'll make a good husband inshAllah.
FAISAL	Thanks Sammy.
ALI	You think I'll make a good husband?

Samina starts laughing.

ALI	What's so funny?
SAMINA	Thought of you as someone's husband.
ALI	What's funny about that? I might be your husband.
SAMINA	You're right, that's not funny at all.
ALI	You like playing hard to get, don't ya?

Beat.

ALI	Why does it have to be a doctor?
SAMINA	Just has to be.
ALI	Us mechanics are better with our hands you know/
SAMINA	Right. That's you done.

ALI   Orrr... I was enjoying that.

SAMINA   Have you got a mirror somewhere?

ALI   Faisal get that wing mirror there.

Faisal gets a broken wing mirror, and gives it to Ali. Samina walks over towards the door.

ALI *(looking in the mirror smiling)* Looks alright actually.

SAMINA   See you later, I'm off to the Demo.

ALI   What?! No you're not.

SAMINA   Try and stop me, princess! Boom! Ha, ha!

Samina leaves, laughing.

ALI   Faisal, stop her for fuck's sake!

Faisal makes an extremely feeble attempt.

FAISAL   Soz bro, she's too fast.

ALI *(panicking)* Fucking hell, get this shit off me! Get me that cloth!

Faisal chucks him an old cloth. Ali wipes off what he can.

ALI   Is it off?!

FAISAL   Not all of it.

ALI   Fuck's sake!

He keeps trying, then gives up.

ALI   What about now?

FAISAL   No.

ALI   Oh fuck this! *(He chucks the cloth)* Let's go!

Ali and Faisal chase after her.

SCENE 3

Shazad's Garage. Same day. 3pm. Ali and Samina return to the garage elated from their counter demo against the English Defence. Faisal with a look of concern.

SAMINA   So bloody proud of Bradfordians today!

ALI   Best Eid ever!

FAISAL   You see that bloke/

SAMINA   The horrids had a wasted trip. Love this city.

ALI   Your speech Sammy!

SAMINA *(enjoying the praise)* So you keep saying.

ALI   Serious Sammy!

SAMINA   Have to stand up and defend our city. Saw what happened in 2001.

ALI   Never forget it.

SAMINA   English Defence should be made to pick up all the police horse shit.

ALI   Give 'em summat to do.

SAMINA   With or without Tommy Powell, they'll never stand a chance against this city if people come out like that/

FAISAL   Guys/

ALI   I'm telling ya Sammy, you fucking killed it! I was cheering like mad after every sentence.

SAMINA   I was only saying what I felt from the heart. If you're passionate about summat it comes out.

ALI   Even Faisal was excited. Jumping up and down like a twat.

FAISAL   Guys.

SAMINA	What is it Faisal?
FAISAL	You see that bloke behind us?
SAMINA	No.
ALI	Surprised me how many non-Muslims were there.
SAMINA	*Everyone* knows the English Defence are just a fascist, racist organization.
ALI	Still surprised me.
SAMINA	Why?
ALI	Most English folk in this country think the same way. Just afraid to say it.
SAMINA	What do you expect when you're flooded with 'evil Muslims' on the news.
ALI	We need to get *you* on the news!
SAMINA	I have been getting a few funny looks lately.
ALI	Coz of your hijab! Forget what happened to that girl/
FAISAL	Girl T.
ALI	Or any terrorist attack... even if no Muslim had done any of that... they'd still look at you with hatred. Coz of your hijab. They want you to wear a short skirt... then they'll be happy. They have no respect for women here... women are treated like sex objects here. In order to sell a Snickers bar... strip a woman naked... need to sell a car? ... Strip a woman naked.
SAMINA	Works, doesn't it?
ALI	Look at all these singers! Miley Cyrus 'n that... no clothes... lickin' sledgehammers.
SAMINA	Wouldn't quite work with a Burka on.

ALI	Anyway forget that shit. I think you should go into politics.
SAMINA	You're over-eggin' it now.
ALI	Serious Sammy. You were fucking awesome out there! Weren't she Fes?
FAISAL	He's right. I could never do summat like that.
ALI	You should definitely go into politics. Media. Shit like that. Need good spokespeople like you. Whenever the media interview someone on the Muslim side, they always pick the worst fucking person... like Faisal here... who hasn't got very good English... who can't explain himself very good... and they give him five seconds... and in that five seconds he's gone 'Errr ... errr... but... but... that's not right'. Then that's it... they cut him off.
SAMINA	There's some intelligent Muslim voices out there now.
ALI	That Mehdi Hassan guy!
FAISAL	Yeah!
ALI	That brother can kill with words.
SAMINA	I'd marry that man.
ALI	He's not a doctor.
SAMINA	That's irrelevant when it comes to him.
FAISAL	Yeah, that Mehdi guy is the business, man. Don't understand what he's saying sometimes... but a' still agree with it.
ALI	He should be Prime Minister man.
SAMINA	I'd vote for him.
ALI	Then he can establish Sharia law.

SAMINA	Don't be stupid, Ali.
ALI	It's the Muslim way.
SAMINA	You're in Britain... you're British.
ALI	You saying Sharia is wrong?
SAMINA	Don't piss me off, Ali. No Muslim country can implement it in the right way. You've no idea of what it is anyway.
ALI	Alright Sammy, you made a good speech in town. Now go back to your lipstick.
SAMINA	You want me to quiz you? Coz I will embarrass you, Ali. In front of Faisal here.
ALI	Shut up.
SAMINA	Most of the leaders in countries enforcing Sharia law haven't even been elected... they've no legitimacy in the first place to implement it. No wonder so many of these countries are fucked up.
ALI	It's Britain and America responsible for that.
SAMINA	At least we're allowed to build mosques here. Practise our religion. We have to respect the laws of the land. This is our Sharia.
ALI	Don't be fucking stupid!
SAMINA	Well fuck off to Saudi then!
ALI	You're talking shit. They'll have laws here soon banning the hijab... will you say it's Sharia then? They'll ban halal meat. They've already got a problem with us building mosques... they din't allow a mosque to be built in New York.
SAMINA	Blame bin Laden.

ALI	Oh come on Sammy, everyone knows 9/11 was an inside job. It was all set up. For all we know Bush and bin Laden were probably sitting together sipping champagne and eating Samosay.
SAMINA	You got photo evidence?
ALI	There's no evidence bin Laden did it. Look... The plane hits it at the top... not even a third of the infrastructure is damaged... and then all of a sudden it comes down like a demolition project... you tell me yeah, which sane person would believe that?!
FAISAL	Ma dad said that Diana's death was not an accident.
ALI	Course it wasn't!
FAISAL	She was killed... coz she was going out with a Muslim... and if she had a kid, it'd be Muslim... who might be like the king 'n that.
ALI	Ya dad's right... Inside job. Why haven't they got to the bottom of that case?!
SAMINA	You guys need to stop reading the Pindu [Simpleton/Villager] Times.

Andy enters.

ALI	Sorry mate we're closed.

Andy is very upset. Shaking.

ALI	Mate. You alright?
ANDY	Fucking Muslim scum.
ALI *(taken aback)*	What?
ANDY	How much do you expect us to take?
ALI	What the fuck did you say?

ANDY   I saw you *(pointing at Samina)* calling us racists... fascists... and *you (pointing at Ali)* shouting 'Allah-hu Akbar' ... stupid grin on your face.

ALI   Best get out of here punk before I smash your fucking face.

ANDY   What's racist about highlighting the issue of young white girls being groomed by grown Muslim men?

ALI   Get the fuck out of here now!

ANDY   Our girls are not halal meat.

ALI   Last warning you white fuck.

ANDY   I'm sick of hearing about how you're a peaceful fucking religion, when all you do is pollute our landscape with your fucking mosques to recruit more of your fuckers to blow this country to smithereens!

Ali goes at Andy, grabbing him.

ANDY *(as they struggle)* Islam is a fucking disease!

SAMINA   Ali!!

Ali finally pushes Andy to the floor. He hits his head on the way down.

ALI   You fucking piece of racist... *(realising Andy's not moving)*

All watch Andy who lies unconscious.

SAMINA *(stunned)* Oh my God, Ali.

SCENE 4

Shazad's Garage. Same day, Evening. The boys are working out using boxing gloves and pads. Shaz is practising combinations, with Ali holding the pads, pausing occasionally. Faisal is watching.

SHAZ   So I had to stand up like this... him sat on the sofa... and recite the full namaaz [prayer] to his face!

Ali and Faisal laugh.

ALI   Embarrassing as fuck, man!

SHAZ   Then he wanted to see me do all the *actions*.

ALI   I better start practising.

SHAZ   Told me I was positioning ma feet wrong during sajda [a prayer position].

FAISAL   Did he let you see her after that?

SHAZ   Yep.

FAISAL   He's good with dads.

ALI   He's not marrying the dad, Fes. Did you save some charm for naughty Naila?

SHAZ   You can just call her 'Naila'.

FAISAL   What was she like?

SHAZ   MashAllah, nice smile.

FAISAL   MashAllah.

ALI   Nice babilons?

SHAZ   This is why I don't tell you these things.

ALI   Nowt wrong with checking out the full package man. I know you did that bro, don't try 'n be all good Muslim 'n that.

SHAZ   I did notice she had a good figure yeah/

ALI   Go on bro!

SHAZ   MashAllah. I like her a lot. She's perfect... you know.

ALI   When you get married to this Naila, you can
              'nail her'.

SHAZ   I'm gonna punch your face.

Ali laughs.

FAISAL   When you meeting her again?

SHAZ   Her family are coming round for dinner in a
              few days. Gotta sort out my CV for then.

FAISAL *(confused)* What?

SHAZ   Her dad wants to see it.

FAISAL   Really?!

ALI   Course man! In the arranged marriage
              business a CV is how you pull.

FAISAL   What you mean?

ALI   You got an impressive CV, you pull an
              impressive girl. Ya grades are like you got a
              rippling six pack, yeah. Good references...?
              Like you got the smooth talk.

FAISAL   Really?

ALI   Job experience...? Like you got the dollars.

FAISAL   I don't have no CV.

ALI   And a master's degree is like you got a big
              dick.

FAISAL   I don't have no master's degree.

SHAZ   I could've had a degree, but with dad dying,
              it wasn't in ma kismet [fate].

ALI   Yeah but MashAllah you got this garage.

SHAZ   Losing customers though.

ALI   Still your own business. My CV's shit. Ain't
              gonna pull no kuri [girl] with it. S'like being
              Faisal on the pull in a nightclub.

FAISAL   What you mean?

Ali and Shaz laugh. Faisal doesn't get it, but joins in anyway.

ALI	Hey don't let Sammy meet her bro. She was getting all protective and jealous.
FAISAL	Yeah, she was telling us in town if she treats you bad she'll behead her 'n that! *(Laughs)*
SHAZ	Town?

Beat.

ALI	Just went to Bombay Stores bro. Picked up a scarf for mum.
SHAZ	And Sammy?
ALI	Needed a bit of advice. Colours 'n that.
SHAZ	Told you not to go anywhere near town.
ALI	We din't go right into town bro. You were right... best not to give any attention to that English Defence lot. Just made a quick trip to Bombay Stores man. MashAllah, picked up a nice scarf.
SHAZ	Where is it?
ALI	What?
SHAZ	This scarf. Let's see it.
ALI	I dropped it off to mum on the way back bro. Alhamdullilah, colour really suited her man.
SHAZ	Right. Come on, hold 'em up!

Shaz runs through some combinations.

FAISAL	When can I have a go?
ALI	I'm next, Fes.
FAISAL	You just went before Shaz!

ALI	No I din't. You're having memory problems again.
FAISAL	I'm not having no memory problems alright! You went before Shaz, it's my turn!
ALI	You can hold the pads.
SHAZ	Bloody hell guys. Ali stop fucking about, let him go next.
ALI	Fucking hell.
SHAZ	Here Fes.

He gives Faisal the gloves. Ali remains on the pads. Faisal starts punching away with enthusiasm.

SHAZ	Wonder what happened at that English Defence demo.
ALI	Oh yeah, we saw a bit on the TV earlier man. Usual stuff. Load of racist thugs, drinking heavily, shouting a load of hate, pissing on't street. Typical goray [white people]. Holding banners saying all sorts of shit about Islam, astaghfirullah [I seek forgiveness from Allah]. Some of 'em got into scuffles with police/

FAISAL *(to Ali on pads)* Hold it higher man.

ALI	Some of 'em got arrested.
SHAZ	As long as it's not our lot getting arrested.
ALI	Lots of our lot out there though bro. Peaceful protest man. Just the way you like it.
SHAZ	Right.
ALI	Sufi style.
SHAZ	Shut up.
FAISAL	Hold it higher man!

ALI	I'm holding it high.
FAISAL	You keep droppin' 'em!
ALI	Come on. Give me some Amir Khan speed. Imagine you're punching Tommy Powell.
SHAZ	Where *is* Samina?
ALI	Inside I think. Twittering.
SHAZ	Haven't seen her.

He goes to exit.

ALI	Bro come on. We need to get our strength back after Ramzaan.
SHAZ	I'll leave you girls to it.
ALI	Only done twenty minutes!
SHAZ	I wanna tell Samina about Naila.
ALI	Don't leave me here with Fes man.
SHAZ	I'll come back in a bit.

He leaves.

ALI	Fuck.
FAISAL	What?
ALI *(checking phone)*	Been trying to get hold of Samina. Don't know where the fuck she is.
FAISAL	You said she was twittering.
ALI	I was trying to keep Shaz here you dumb ass.
FAISAL	You think we should tell Shaz what happened?
ALI	You wanna keep your legs?
FAISAL	Shit.
ALI	Yeah, shit.
FAISAL	You think that dude's gonna be alright?

ALI   Doctor said he was fine. Just a little knock on the head man.

FAISAL   Yeah.

ALI   Just hope that girl *is* in her room twittering.

SCENE 5

Same evening. Samina and Andy at the A & E, Bradford Royal Infirmary. Andy has a bandage around his head from the knock. He is waiting for further treatment in the waiting room.

ANDY   I had a business if you must know!

SAMINA   What kind?

ANDY   Halal meat shop.

SAMINA   Fuck off!

Beat.

ANDY   Why so shocked?

Beat.

ANDY   Have to cater for your market, don't you?

SAMINA   Don't believe you.

ANDY   You think I give a shit?

SAMINA   You still got it?

Beat.

ANDY   No.

SAMINA   Crashed and burned?

ANDY   It was doing very well actually! All year round! Didn't sell any pork, halal turkey during Christmas, very popular! Had to stock up with huge amounts of lamb, chicken, beef during Eid... hundreds of customers!

SAMINA   What was it called?

ANDY   Oak Lane Halal Meats.

SAMINA   Don't remember it.

ANDY   You were probably in nappies love.

SAMINA   What happened then?

Beat.

SAMINA *(persistent)* Come on, what happened?

ANDY   It was set alight. During the riots.

SAMINA   Asian thugs?

ANDY   White lads.

SAMINA   Really?!

ANDY   Who thought it was owned by an Asian. Who would think otherwise? They were standing up for the whites in this city. The Asians started it, Muslims. Since then I've watched this country... and the world get attacked and molested by Muslims... sorry if that offends you.

SAMINA   It does/

ANDY   Well, that's how I feel.

SAMINA   Offends me a lot/

ANDY   You're asking the questions luv. I'm just answering.

SAMINA   Typical.

ANDY   What is?

SAMINA   You blame Muslims, even though they had nothing to do with it. And by the way, 'Asian' doesn't necessarily mean 'Muslim'.

ANDY	Most of the Asians in Bradford are of Pakistani heritage. Most of the boys involved in the riots were of Pakistani, *Muslim* background. I'm not a thick skinhead you know. I've read up. I've done my research.
SAMINA	*Daily Mail*?
ANDY	Qur'an.
SAMINA	You've read the Qur'an?
ANDY	English translation.
SAMINA	Like fuck you have.
ANDY	'Bismillah hi rahma ni raheem'.

Beat.

SAMINA	Box of surprises, aren't you?
ANDY	How old are you?
SAMINA	Twenty.
ANDY	Same sort of age as my daughter.
SAMINA	And?
ANDY	It's because of her that I read it.
SAMINA	Why?
ANDY	She's a Muslim.
SAMINA *(shocked)*	What?!
ANDY	Converted. Or 'reverted' as she calls it.

Beat.

SAMINA	What made her convert?
ANDY	Started seeing this Muslim lad. Iqqy was the name. Right before her A-levels.
SAMINA	Right.
ANDY	Few months later, converted. Started wearing the head scarf.

SAMINA	And her father's a member of English Defence. Bet she loves that!
ANDY	Haven't spoken to her for four years.
SAMINA	Because she converted?
ANDY	She was doing well at school... went out with friends... drinking on the town with her mates... clubbing... a normal English lass. Could've gone to university... very bright. That all went down the pan. Told me she'd agreed to marry this Iqqy. I told her to make a choice... him or me.
SAMINA	Did you meet this Iqqy?
ANDY	Refused to meet him. But he approached me in the street one time and tried to introduce himself to me. Wearing that long white thing. Beard, turban. I was thinking fucking hell... my daughter's marrying Osama bin Laden.
SAMINA	What did you say to him?
ANDY	Got in my car and drove off.
SAMINA	So basically, you object to your daughter marrying this man *just* because he's a Muslim?
ANDY	She didn't even sit her A-level exams. Missed out on university... a chance to make something of herself. Now she's married to this Iqqy. Four kids already! Don't even recognize her any more... my own daughter... I don't even know who she is.
SAMINA	She tried to get in touch?
ANDY	Yeah. But I don't answer. She made her choice.

SAMINA	You happy about that?
ANDY	Course I'm not happy!! She's my only daughter! It was my fault running a fucking halal meat shop! Getting her to help me out on her school holidays. Muslim men coming in day after day grooming her.
SAMINA	You really are a wanker, aren't you?
ANDY	You've been pestering me for an hour now. Time you fucked off?
SAMINA	'100% English Defence Loyal'. Nice Twitter biog.
ANDY	Well... no point beating about the bush.
SAMINA	Loyal like Tommy Powell?
ANDY	Don't even mention that cunt's name.
SAMINA	Tommy Powell.
ANDY	Why don't you fuck off home? Back to your five daily prayers.
SAMINA	I'm going nowhere Hitler.
ANDY	Just fuck off!

Silence.

SAMINA	OK. I apologise. No more insults.
ANDY	As if your dad would be happy with you seeing a white boy.

Silence.

SAMINA	You're against Islamic Extremism right?
ANDY	Yeah.
SAMINA	And the sexual exploitation of young girls?
ANDY	Hundred percent.
SAMINA	So am I. I'm inviting you to join a group I formed?

ANDY	Al-Qaeda?
SAMINA	'Bradford for Peace'.
ANDY	A Muslim organization? No thanks.
SAMINA	It's not a Muslim organization. We've got members from all backgrounds, all faiths.
ANDY	No ta.
SAMINA	Just come to one meeting.
ANDY	I said fuck you very much.
SAMINA	We actively go out, speak out against all the issues *you're* against. We're actually *doing* something about it. We're not drinking, singing and dancing around like we're all at a football match/
ANDY	Some of our younger lot might get carried away... we can't control everyone... like at a football match, you get a few hooligans. You don't blame all the supporters.
SAMINA	Don't blame Islam then because of the actions of a few Muslims.
ANDY	Not all Muslims are groomers, but all the groomers just happen to be Muslim. What does that tell you?
SAMINA	Why do you have to bring religion into it? I saw the banners you were all holding, 'Lock up your daughters, the Qur'an is evil'. Throwing around quotes you have no understanding of. It's a *criminal* problem, not a religious one.
ANDY	Well, it might be a religious problem?
SAMINA	Why?

Beat.

ANDY	I've read the Qur'an.

SAMINA   You've said.

Beat.

ANDY   How old was that young girl who your Prophet married?

SAMINA *(shaking her head)* Oh. My. God.

ANDY   How old was she?

SAMINA   You twisted man/

ANDY   I'm just asking a question, a simple question. How old was she? How old was she when he consummated the marriage?

SAMINA   So what you're saying is, that what these men did here in Bradford is linked to the Prophet somehow?

ANDY   How old was she? Simple question/

SAMINA   Nobody knows her age actually! ... Some accounts say she was sixteen or seventeen... but ignorant people use these arguments all the time... when they have no clue about Islam... the Prophet's life... or the history of the period. You have to understand things in the context of the time for fuck's sake! We're talking fourteen hundred years ago... marriage at a younger age was the norm... all over the fucking world... Here too! During the Prophet's time... in *seventh century* Arabia... it was a *legitimate* marriage... and she was the daughter of his closest companion... and no one ever fucking talks about his actual marriage to her! ... Or what Aisha thought... Who was Aisha? ... What did she become? Do you know anything about that?! No you fucking don't! She became a strong... independent...

intelligent... politically aware woman... she became a *prominent political leader*... she was *proud* of her husband until the day he died... she talked about the Prophet with *affection*. Half of what we know about the Prophet is down to her. So you can use your ridiculous arguments to make us all look twisted... but you will always fail, because your ignorance level is off the fucking scale!

Beat.

ANDY I'm not saying he's a paedophile... I'm not saying that at all. But having sex with a child today is classed as paedophilia. And some people might take your Prophet's marriage to Aisha to allow them to have sex with kids.

SAMINA So you're saying that those groomers did what they did because they were following Islam?

ANDY You're misunderstanding what I'm saying.

SAMINA Well, what are you saying?

ANDY I'm just saying some Muslims might interpret it the wrong way.

SAMINA If there is anyone who thinks that they can rape and abuse a young child, they should be severely punished! It is *utterly* and *completely* against the teachings of Islam to do anything like that. I wouldn't be a proud Muslim if my religion encouraged any practise like that, you ignorant plonker!

Silence.

ANDY When do you have this 'Bradford for Peace' meeting?

SCENE 6

Ali and Samina. Samina's house. Kitchen. Same evening. 11pm.

SAMINA   I went back.

ALI   What?!

SAMINA   To the hospital.

ALI   What the fuck, why?!

SAMINA   He's agreed to come to the next BFP meeting.

ALI   You went to see that racist fuck and now he's going to one of your meetings?!

SAMINA   Keep your voice down. Mum's in the next room.

ALI   Why?! How?!

SAMINA   Keep your voice down!

ALI   Shaz is driving around looking for you!

SAMINA   Shit.

ALI   Yes, shit! If he finds out about this you'll be in a coffin.

SAMINA   The guy's harmless.

ALI   You're crazy, Sammy.

SAMINA   Why have you started being all goody two-shoes?

ALI   I almost killed the benchoud!

SAMINA   Don't worry, he's not gonna report it.

ALI   Don't give a fuck. If he comes anywhere near here again I'll finish him off.

SAMINA   The Qur'an says create dialogue with people, especially those you disagree with.

	It promises you'll be pleasantly surprised... and that you might become good friends.
ALI	Yeah, I'm picturing you having a pint with your racist pal down the pub.
SAMINA	Think about how the Prophet, peace be upon him, would have done things.
ALI	Slay those who attack Islam. That's what it says in the Qur'an.
SAMINA	Really?!
ALI	Summat like that.
SAMINA	You haven't even read the Qur'an Ali.
ALI	Shut up.
SAMINA	Mr expert on Islam, hasn't even read the Qur'an.

ALI *(embarrassed)* Shut the fuck up, alright.

Beat.

SAMINA	He's not a bad person. Just ignorant. Angry about Girl T. I'm angry about that too. So we've got that in common. We both want to stop these dirty paedophile rapists grooming young girls. And I'm *ashamed* that our *Pakistani, Muslim* men are doing this and dragging our reputation, and the reputation of Islam through the mud. You know another sick bastard was arrested today?

ALI *(worried)* Who? The uncle who ran off to Pakistan?

SAMINA	Someone else. Another sick Paki.
ALI	Really?
SAMINA	Paid to have sex with her.
ALI	What's his name?

SAMINA	I don't know. But 'Sick Fuck' might be a good one.
ALI	What paper was/
SAMINA	A *forty*-odd man paid to have sex with a *twelve* year old. Apparently there's more of these sick paedos out there. Police are gonna hunt down every single one.

Terror in Ali's eyes.

ALI	I blame the parents.
SAMINA	What?
ALI	If it was *my* daughter I wun't have let her out the house.
SAMINA	What about the groomers, you don't blame them?
ALI	No.
SAMINA	You don't blame the dirty old sick bastards who took advantage of a girl who's not even a teenager?
ALI	No.
SAMINA	Get out, Ali.
ALI	I'm only winding you up.
SAMINA	Get out!
ALI	Why are these English girls out at two in the morning, you asked yourself that?
SAMINA	So it's the victim's fault? A twelve year old victim?
ALI	Apnay [our] girls aren't even allowed out after six.
SAMINA	You're making me sick.
ALI	Your bro looks after you the right way.
SAMINA	Go!

ALI	You meet this guy again, I'm telling Shaz.
SAMINA	Fucking go on then!
ALI	Qur'an-ay-kasme I will.
SAMINA	You'd be in shit too.
ALI	Not as much shit as you. You'll have to do all your political speeches to the bedroom wall. See you later Wonder Woman.

He exits.

Interval.

SCENE 7

Four days later. 11th August. Andy has just attended the BFP meeting at Frizinghall Community Centre. All have left apart from Samina and Andy. Samina is trying to encourage Andy to sing the song the group have just created together. (See link for the song: http://vimeo. com/27530154).

SAMINA	*We're Bradford People,*
	We've come together,
	We want peace, we want peace,
	We want peace, peace, peace,
	No aggression,
	No provocation,
	So let's keep Bradford peaceful now.
	Come on. Have a go.
ANDY	I'm not singing it.
SAMINA	Come on.
ANDY	No chance.
SAMINA	You just helped create the lyrics.
ANDY	I said no.
SAMINA	I'll sing it with you.

ANDY   I'm not the singing type alright.

SAMINA   You sang all the English Defence chants, I bet.

ANDY   Stuff your BFP, I'm off! *(He turns to leave)*

SAMINA   I'm sorry! Bloody hell. We won't sing, alright?

ANDY   Good.

Beat.

SAMINA   So what d'you think? Saw you chatting to people?

ANDY   Did you tell 'em I was part of English Defence?

SAMINA   Best not to mention that I reckon.

ANDY   Right.

SAMINA   So what you think?

ANDY   It's a bit... girly.

SAMINA   Well, most of our members are women, but we're trying to get more men involved.

ANDY   Right.

SAMINA   Had a very productive meeting I reckon. The song was a brilliant idea! Could start all our meetings with that. Don't worry, I won't force you. Be great to sing it as a group on Centenary Square. Get the public to join us! And the ribbons! Everyone wears a ribbon. Simple, but powerful!

ANDY   Not really my colour, lime green.

SAMINA   Great brainstorming session about how we can unite the city again. Talks in schools. Girl T's school. Irfaan's idea about making a video about the group/

ANDY	I suggested that idea actually.
SAMINA	Sorry your idea. Great suggestion.
ANDY	I've got camcorder experience.
SAMINA	What?
ANDY	Family videos.
SAMINA	Nice one.
ANDY	My daughter's Christening. Parties. Things like that.
SAMINA	Great!
ANDY	'They look professional'.
SAMINA	What?
ANDY	It's what people used to say.
SAMINA	Really?
ANDY	Yeah.
SAMINA	Some funding might be helpful.
ANDY	I've got some ideas for that.
SAMINA	Great. You can share it with us next time.
ANDY	Yeah.
SAMINA	We've got a news reporter coming next time. T & A.
ANDY	Help get the word out.
SAMINA	Totally.
ANDY	Yeah, be good to speak to 'em.
SAMINA	So you'll come again?
ANDY	Well, you need more men don't you?
SAMINA	We do! *(Suddenly remembering the time)* Oh shit. What's the time? *(Pulls out her phone)* Shit!
ANDY	What?
SAMINA	Twelve missed calls. Fuck.

ANDY	Who from?
SAMINA	Brother. Told him I'd be home before nine.
ANDY	You're not doing anything wrong. What's the panic?
SAMINA	He's just become stupidly over-protective lately.
ANDY	I see.
SAMINA	And he's got marriage plans on the go. The potential wife and in-laws came over for dinner last night. I had to be a good little girl.
ANDY	A 'good little girl'?
SAMINA	You know... be good etcetera.
ANDY	Arranged thing is it?
SAMINA	Yeah. But I think he's in love. Hormones all over the place.
ANDY	Right.
SAMINA	I better go.
ANDY	Yeah I can see that.

Samina, flustered, gathers her things.

SAMINA	I was thinking Andy... about your daughter.
ANDY	Yes?
SAMINA	Four years is a long time.
ANDY	It is.
SAMINA	Do you have any other family?
ANDY	Her mother died seven years ago.
SAMINA	Really sorry to hear that.
ANDY	Yeah.
SAMINA	You should call her, you know?
ANDY	Rather not talk about it.

SAMINA   You've got grandkids.

ANDY   None of your business.

SAMINA   I know it isn't but/

ANDY   Your brother will be getting anxious.

Beat.

SAMINA   Yeah. *(Samina turns to go)*

ANDY   I do love her, you know.

SAMINA   Yeah.

ANDY   I'm not a heartless bastard.

SAMINA   I know.

ANDY   She's a bit like you actually.

SAMINA   Really?

ANDY   Full of life in the eyes. Hard work. She stopped eating at one point. Anorexia. Her mother dying was a big blow to her. I was convinced it was because of that, but she told me later that her fucking teacher at school said she had 'fat legs'. I went mad. Stormed into her school. Almost hit the woman.

SAMINA   Did she get better?

ANDY   Yeah. But it took a long time helping her through it. Did incredibly well at her GSCEs. Four A's.

SAMINA   I'm glad.

ANDY   You better go.

SAMINA   See you in a couple of days, Andy.

ANDY   Yeah.

Samina exits.

SCENE 8

Same evening. 10.45pm. Shazad's Garage. Faisal has just come from the mosque in a panic. A brick was thrown through the mosque window during the Maghrib [sunset] prayer.

SHAZ   Alright, calm down Fes. Just tell us *everything*, right from the *beginning*.

FAISAL   I'd just... I'd just finished eating a Big Dripper Burger with fries/

SHAZ   I mean from the beginning when you were at the mosque.

FAISAL   Oh... erm... we were in the middle of doing our namaaz 'n that... doing that last rakhat [prayer cycle]... and before we knew it a massive brick smashed through the window!

ALI   Fucking hell.

SHAZ   Was anybody hurt?

FAISAL   Yeah. One guy was hit on the shoulder. The ambulance came 'n that. Police.

ALI   Who's the terrorist now ey?!

SHAZ   Anyone else? Were you hurt?

FAISAL   No. But there was loads of glass all over the floor 'n that. I had bare feet. I could have standed on it!

ALI   Loads more could have been hurt. Killed. Murdered. This is attempted murder.

SHAZ   Did anyone see who did it?

ALI   We know exactly who it is!

FAISAL	No coz we were all inside. But two Sikh guys came in to see if we were OK. Helped the injured guy 'n that.
SHAZ	Good on 'em.
FAISAL	Oh and apparently there was a note on the brick.
ALI	Yeah?
FAISAL	It said 'This is for Girl T'.
ALI	Fucking English Defence. I'm gonna kill 'em!
SHAZ	Well, let's thank Allah no one was hurt.
ALI	What next?! A fucking petrol bomb?!
SHAZ	Chill out, Ali.
ALI	Shall we take 'em some tea 'n biscuits now Shaz?
SHAZ	Knobhead.
FAISAL	It's prob'ly coz another Pakistani guy was arrested today for the Girl T thing.
SHAZ	Another one?!
ALI	Who? The uncle?
FAISAL	No. Zeeshan summat. Paid to have sex with her 'n that.
SHAZ	Unbelievable.
FAISAL	Said on the news there's still more of 'em who did that.
SHAZ	Fucking shameful.
ALI *(changing the subject)* Where's Samina?
SHAZ	I've been trying to ring her God knows how many times. Not answering her fucking phone!
ALI	She shouldn't be out bro. It's not safe.

SHAZ	Not safe for any Muslim coz of these rapist cunts.
ALI	Bell her again.

Shaz tries calling her again as Samina walks in.

SHAZ	Where the fuck were you?!
SAMINA	Soz bhai. Bus didn't turn up for ages. I was at Hannah's.
SHAZ	You know what's just happened?!
SAMINA	What?
SHAZ	Our mosque was attacked! Faisal was there!
SAMINA	Oh my God! How?
FAISAL	A brick.
SAMINA	You alright, Fes?
FAISAL	Yeah. All praises to Allah. But there was loads of broken glass on the floor and I had bare feet/
SHAZ	Why din't you answer your phone?

FAISAL *(to Samina)* ... I could've standed on it.

SAMINA	I was doing my assignment with Hannah.

FAISAL *(to Samina)* ... It was very sharp glass.

SHAZ	I told you to always keep your phone on!
SAMINA	Sorry bhai.
SHAZ	From now on I'm dropping you off and picking you up every time you leave the house.
SAMINA	You don't have to do that.
SHAZ	I wanna know *exactly* where you are. *Always.*
SAMINA	Bhai, you don't need to treat me like/
ALI	Listen to your bro Sammy.

Beat.

SAMINA   Fine.

SHAZ   Ali. Walk her to the house.

ALI   Right. *(To Samina)* Come on.

Ali exits with Samina.

SCENE 9

Shazad's Garage. 3 days later. 14th Aug. Morning.

FAISAL   My dad asked me last night if I wanted to marry my cousin in Pakistan.

SHAZ   Really?

FAISAL   Yeah.

SHAZ   And?

FAISAL   Also...

SHAZ   What?

FAISAL   If I wanted to move there and join the family business 'n that.

SHAZ   Right.

FAISAL   I said yes.

SHAZ   Right. *(Beat)* Mubarak Faisal. *(Beat)* Is that what you want?

FAISAL   I don't know bro. *(Beat)* It's what ma dad wants 'n that.

SHAZ   Don't just do it coz your dad wants it.

FAISAL   It'd be safer in Pakistan.

SHAZ   In what way?

FAISAL   Everyone's Muslim innit. No Islamophobia 'n that.

SHAZ   Technically it's not safe.

FAISAL   What you mean?

SHAZ   Well, extremists are suicide bombing it... and America are drone attacking it.

FAISAL   I was thinking...

SHAZ   What?

FAISAL   I was thinking about... like... what if Tommy Powell became the Prime Minister 'n that... and then made a law against all us Muslims... and we all had to like... leave 'n that... to another country.

SHAZ   Scary thought, Faisal.

FAISAL   It might be like a Holocraft.

SHAZ   Holocaust?

FAISAL   Yeah, Holocaust.

SHAZ   Faisal, there's more chance of Tommy Powell becoming leader of Al Qaeda.

FAISAL   Yeah.

SHAZ   You can't just move to Pakistan and marry your cousin coz you're scared of living here.

FAISAL   Yeah...

SHAZ   It's not a great time for Muslims... but it's a test... from Allah... it's up to us to make it different.

FAISAL   Yeah but... I can't do that.

SHAZ   What?

FAISAL   I'm not like you guys bro.

SHAZ   What you mean?

Beat.

FAISAL   Last night after ma dad asked me about ma cousin... my uncle came over... he told him I said yes... they were happy 'n that.

Then they were watching the news and it was talking about a gay man who had been attacked 'n that... had his toes hammered by this guy. They were laughing about it and saying things I didn't agree with... but I was laughing with 'em you know... I was too scared to say what I thought.

SHAZ Alright.

FAISAL I'm a little bit stupid I think.

SHAZ You're a fucking brilliant mechanic Fes... better than me!

FAISAL Right.

SHAZ He's your dad... but that doesn't mean he's always right... you've got your own mind Fes... your own opinions... just as valid as anybody else... just open your mouth and say 'em.

FAISAL Yeah but ma dad will never understand... he'll just tell me what's Islamic and what's not.

SHAZ You mean what *he* thinks is Islamic.

FAISAL Right.

SHAZ I mean... no disrespect to your dad... I know he means a lot to you... but just because he's got a beard, carries a thasbi [prayer beads] around and owns some leather socks... doesn't mean he's an expert on Islam.

FAISAL You think my dad's a bad Muslim.

SHAZ Nah Fes... I'm not saying that. But from the sounds of it... he wasn't being very Islamic last night.

FAISAL Yeah.

SHAZ I think you should tell your dad 'no'.

FAISAL   What?

SHAZ   Tell him you don't wanna move to Pakistan and marry your cousin. You've got a permanent job here with me.

Ali walks in with a newspaper in hand.

FAISAL   I can't do that bro.

ALI   Can't do what?

SHAZ   You're late.

ALI   Soz bro. Had another yelling competition with dad.

SHAZ   Right.

ALI *(showing the newspaper article)* Look what I found here. Smallest article in the whole paper. I wonder why.

SHAZ *(reads)* 'Another man arrested in connection with the Girl T inquiry'.

ALI   Another *white* man. Craig Fletcher!

SHAZ   Really?

ALI   A non-Muslim. Fucking yes!

SHAZ   Nothing to celebrate Ali.

ALI   These English Defence fuckers blaming us Muslims for this shit... smashing our mosques... and it's one of them!

SHAZ   Guess it proves it's not just a Muslim problem.

ALI   You bet it does bro! You bet it does.

SHAZ   We got a visit from 'Saltaire Taxis'. Need to do a service on three of their cars. Could lead to more work, so come on, grab your overalls.

ALI   Right boss.

Shaz's phone rings.

SHAZ *(in the tone of a man in love)* Hiya... Assalaamu-alaycum.

ALI 'Hiya... Assalaamu-alaycum' *(Laughs)* You know who lover boy's speaking to with that voice.

FAISAL Who?

ALI Dumb twat.

SHAZ No... No I haven't seen it. What?! ... I can't believe this... what page? Right... let me call you back.

ALI What is it?

SHAZ Gimme that paper.

Ali passes over the paper. Shaz opens up on the page Naila mentioned.

ALI What is it?

Shaz storms out, furious.

SCENE 10

Samina's bedroom. Shaz holds a newspaper article with a photograph of Samina and Andy together.

SHAZ What's this?! *(No response. Shaz reads the article)* 'Muslim student teams up with English Defence member to tackle Islamic street grooming.' *(Beat)* Naila's dad's seen it.

SAMINA And?

SHAZ He's cancelled the engagement.

SAMINA What?!

SHAZ	Doesn't want anything to do with us anymore.
SAMINA	That's ridiculous!
SHAZ	What's ridiculous is you associating with someone from the English Defence?!
SAMINA	He's not a member anymore.
SHAZ	I don't give a shit.
SAMINA	We're both trying to do a good thing. Can't believe he doesn't want anything to do with us because of that!
SHAZ *(reads a quote from Andy)*	'I believe the Qur'an needs to be reformed. Take the hateful verses out of the book. Terrorists and paedophiles are using verses from the Qur'an to justify their actions. It needs to be modernised.'

Beat.

SAMINA	I had no idea he said that.
SHAZ	If you've ruined my chances with Naila/
SAMINA	I'll call her family.
SHAZ	Where d'you meet this guy?

Beat.

SAMINA	At the demo.
SHAZ	The demo I told you not to go to?
SAMINA	Yeah.
SHAZ	Did Ali and Faisal go?
SAMINA	Yeah.
SHAZ	Get used to your bedroom coz you'll be going nowhere now.
SAMINA	Bhai/

SHAZ	Don't give me any excuses alright! You don't listen to a word I say. I've worked my arse off since dad died... trying to look after you and mum. I finally meet someone I really like and you fuck it up!
SAMINA	I'll speak to Naila's family. Explain.
SHAZ	You're not going back to that group.
SAMINA	Yes I am.
SHAZ	You're gonna fucking stay in the house!! You hear me?!
SAMINA	There's not enough Muslims speaking up! They just brush these issues under the fucking carpet! I'm trying to make a change... trying to show that I'm a Muslim fighting the same battle. All the Pakis in this town wanna sit in their little houses... do their regular back-biting about their neighbours kids. But when we do have a serious problem, where the fuck are they?! Islam is in a mess in this country... no one has anything good to say about us. We've got some so-called Muslim paedo rapists out there! I have to suffer the backlash of this shit! I'm embarrassed to say I'm Muslim these days. It's the worst thing to be right now. If we don't actively do something about it... make ourselves heard/ (then things are never gonna change)
SHAZ	I'm one of those 'Pakis' am I?
SAMINA	If you don't speak up you're contributing to the problem.
SHAZ	I'm contributing to the problem by trying to live a stress free life? Look after my family?

SAMINA   I haven't read that article but sounds like its been written by an ignorant wanker. '*Islamic* grooming'?!

SHAZ   You're not stepping foot out of this house until you go back to Uni.

SAMINA   What?!

SHAZ   That's right.

SAMINA   Please bhai.

SHAZ *(threatening)* I'm this close from pulling you out of Uni altogether. Don't push me.

SAMINA   OK.

SHAZ   I promised dad before he died that I'd look after you and mum. And that's what I'm gonna do. Stay put. This is the last time I tell you. I fucking mean it.

He exits.

SCENE 11

Following day. 12pm. Samina and Andy meet in a café.

ANDY   It's what I believe.

SAMINA   I was sitting there, agreeing with everything you were saying... and then you go and tell the reporter something like that?!

ANDY   Samina. If it says in a book, 'You're allowed to do X' and then people who follow that book go out and do X, of course it is that book's fault.

SAMINA   You're just going to wind up every Muslim who would have given us support.

ANDY   I'm just saying there are verses in the Qur'an that need to be explored, because

Islamists are using those verses to justify what they do. I don't see why those verses can't be removed.

SAMINA People need to stop being so ignorant and do some fucking research. Understand what Islam's actually about.

ANDY Tell that to bin Laden. Well not bin Laden, he's dead. Tell that to Anjem Choudary.

SAMINA You do know about the white, non-Muslim arrested yesterday?

ANDY Some people are suggesting he might have been a convert.

SAMINA That's bullshit!

ANDY It's what people are saying.

SAMINA Which people?

ANDY People.

SAMINA You've caused me a lot of hassle at home, Andy.

ANDY How?

SAMINA I'm having to sneak out.

ANDY Why?

SAMINA Because my brother now knows who I'm hanging out with.

ANDY You're not allowed out because of him?

SAMINA Yes.

ANDY Very controlling, your brother, isn't he?

SAMINA He's trying to protect me.

ANDY Did he force you to wear your niqab?

SAMINA No he didn't!

ANDY Alright, no need to shout.

SAMINA And it's a hijab!

ANDY	'Hijab' then.
SAMINA	I thought we were moving forward.
ANDY	My views are my views.
SAMINA	Well, just keep the Islamophobic ones to yourself.
ANDY	Fine.
SAMINA	Fine.
ANDY	But they're not Islamophobic.
SAMINA	They are.
ANDY	I think there needs to be some kind of documentary programme, which explores the Qur'an, page by page, and explains to everyone what each verse is about. Then there'll be no confusion or misunderstanding from either side.
SAMINA	Maybe.
ANDY	I could make it. With my camcorder experience.
SAMINA	Why not.
ANDY	A friend of mine knows someone who's got a connection with that Amanda Holden from... err... what you call it? *Britain's Got Talent*.
SAMINA	What the fuck does she know about Islam?!
ANDY	She might be able to get us in with the BBC.
SAMINA	Right now, the BBC are too busy! Demonizing Muslims left, right and centre. We're the targets. It used to be the blacks, the Jews, the Irish, the homosexuals... now it's our turn. People can now say things about Muslims they wouldn't dare say about blacks, Jews or homosexuals.

ANDY Rubbish. Newspapers wouldn't dare say anything about Muhammed. They're terrified.

SAMINA Just look on Facebook, Twitter. Comment after comment, people bashing Islam. Bashing me... basically. The word 'Islamophobia' didn't even exist a few years ago.

ANDY But a few suicide bombings later...

SAMINA *I'm* not safe from terrorist attacks either you know. They don't discriminate who they're gonna kill when they decide to blow up a bus... and then because of these attacks *I'm* demonized by the media and everyone... have to worry about reprisal attacks, bricks through mosque windows. My brother prays at that mosque you know.

ANDY People are angry.

SAMINA I'm proud of being British... I love my country... but when I hear and read Islamophobic comments, *constantly*... it makes me question... do I really belong here? It seriously gets me down. It really gets me down.

Beat.

ANDY No you're right. That's not fair.

Beat.

SAMINA So anyway. Lets focus on the things we have in common. Not what divides us.

ANDY I'm with that.

SAMINA I've been in touch with local schools. They were happy to hear from me... three of 'em said we can visit first term after their summer holiday. Lots to speak about. Have to protect these girls. I wanna visit as many schools as possible. We don't want this horror happening to anyone else. Meanwhile, Irfaan said he wanted to talk to Muslim boys directly in mosques, educate them about Islam and women.

ANDY   Sounds like a plan.

SAMINA   Good.

Beat.

ANDY *(sings very quietly so only Samina can hear)* We're Bradford People,
We've come together,
We want peace, we want peace,
We want peace, peace, peace,
No aggression,
No provocation,
So let's keep Bradford peaceful now.

SAMINA   You're singing it!

ANDY   Been practising.

SAMINA   I'm proud.

ANDY   I called Louise.

SAMINA   Who?

ANDY   Well 'Mariam' now that she's changed her name.

SAMINA   That's great news!

ANDY   Thanks.

SAMINA   And?

Beat.

ANDY   She's still a Muslim.

SCENE 12

Shazad's Garage. 2 days later. 17th Aug. Evening. Ali enters the garage on his own. He has a large suitcase with him. He sits on his case. After a few seconds Samina enters, in tears.

SAMINA   Where's bhai-jaan?

ALI   Romantic meal with Naila. *(Noticing)* What's wrong?

Samina is so upset she can't speak.

ALI   Sammy... what's happened?

SAMINA   Girl T. On the news. Committed suicide.

ALI   What?!

SAMINA   Overdose.

ALI   Fucking hell.

SAMINA   She was called Tracy.

Samina in tears. Ali walks over to Samina.

ALI   Come on. Come here.

Ali hugs Samina. She cries.

ALI   That's fucked up news, Sammy.

SAMINA   She was recovering. Getting better. Then this.

ALI   That's real fucked up.

SAMINA   I wish I could have helped her.

ALI   You're a special girl, Sammy.

SAMINA   It's made me even more determined to do something about this shit. Those so-called Muslim bastards. Those sick fuckers did this to her! I feel like I could kill 'em! All of 'em!

ALI	Come on Sammy.
SAMINA	I'm gonna fucking kill 'em Ali.
ALI	It's alright Sammy. It's alright.

They hug. After a while Samina notices Ali's large suitcase.

SAMINA	Is that yours?
ALI	Yep.
SAMINA	Why? Where you going?
ALI	Been chucked out.
SAMINA	What?!
ALI	Dad said get out. So I packed ma stuff.
SAMINA	Why?
ALI	You know what it's like.
SAMINA	Yeah, but this.
ALI	It's alright. I'm gonna ask Shaz if I can sleep in here for a while.
SAMINA	Mum won't allow that. You'll have to stay at ours.
ALI	Here's perfect. Done it before. Look. I can choose any car I want! Kip on't back seat.
SAMINA	No Ali. That's ridiculous. We've got a spare room.
ALI	We'll see. I'll speak to Shaz.
SAMINA	You have to go back. Patch things up.
ALI	It's past that, Sammy.
SAMINA	Ali, he's your dad. You've *got* a dad. I'd do anything to have my dad back. I know your dad. I know how much he cares about you.
ALI	I've done some bad things.
SAMINA	You were a teenager then.

ALI	Not just the robbery. Other things. Bad things.
SAMINA	We all make mistakes. But you know, Allah will always forgive you. You just have to ask for forgiveness.
ALI	Ma dad's still not forgiven me.
SAMINA	He just wants to be proud of his son.
ALI	He's proud of his best mate's son more than his own. He told me that he went to Shaz in tears and literally begged him to give me a job in this garage... and to 'guide me along the straight path'.
SAMINA	Really?
ALI	You think he employed me for my skills under the bonnet?
SAMINA	Shaz isn't perfect either. After dad died, he had no choice. He had to be responsible.
ALI	I liked your dad.
SAMINA	I miss him.
ALI	He stuck up for me.
SAMINA	You were like another son to him, you know.
ALI	It's important I have his approval.
SAMINA	Why?
ALI	I wanna marry you.
SAMINA	Shut up, Ali.
ALI	I'm serious, Sammy.

Beat.

SAMINA	You serious?
ALI	Deadly serious. *(Beat)* Look I know I'm no doctor. I know you're out of my league.

Educated 'n that. But I'll be a good husband to you, Sammy. I'll sort myself out, good and proper. With you as my wife, I can do anything. I'll start praying five times a day. I'll make summat of myself. Make you proud. It'll make my dad proud! Trust me. I promise you on my mum's life I'll make you happy and take care of you. *(Beat)* I've loved you for years, Sammy. *(Beat)* I wanted to ask Shaz first you know. Do it the right way. Islamic. *(Beat)* What do you think Sammy?

Beat.

SAMINA   Bloody hell, Ali. *(Beat)* I'm still at Uni. Mum's not even spoken to me about marriage yet.

ALI   I'll wait. I'm willing to wait.

Silence. Samina doesn't know how to respond.

SAMINA   OK.

ALI   OK what?

Faisal enters.

SAMINA   Faisal.

FAISAL   Oh there you are. There's a couple of coppers outside you know. Want to speak to Ali.

SCENE 13

Two weeks later. Shazad's Garage. Shaz is wearing a suit, reading the Qur'an. The garage is empty. It's been closed down. Samina enters.

SAMINA	You've been here hours bhai. *(No response)* Mum says come in. Dinner's made.
SHAZ	In a bit.

Beat.

SAMINA	You had absolutely nothing to do with it.
SHAZ	He paid two hundred pounds for it.
SAMINA	What?
SHAZ	Two hundred pounds to...
SAMINA	I'm sickened.
SHAZ	Wages I had given him.
SAMINA	How d'you know?
SHAZ	Faisal. He went this morning with his dad. Ali pleaded guilty. He was crying. Said he din't know she was twelve.
SAMINA	Do you believe him?
SHAZ	I don't know.
SAMINA	So if she was sixteen it would be acceptable? Which part of the fucking equation did he think *was* acceptable?
SHAZ	I know.
SAMINA	I mean... what the fuck...
SHAZ	I know. I know.
SAMINA	I just can't get my head around it. I can't believe I could trust someone like that. I just...
SHAZ	You think I should've gone?
SAMINA	His dad went. So did Faisal.
SHAZ	I just couldn't go.
SAMINA	How long?
SHAZ	What?

SAMINA   The sentence?

SHAZ   A long time.

SAMINA   He's destroyed his parents. Mum's been round there again to see 'em. They don't know what to do. Daren't leave the house. They were talking about moving to Pakistan. I think that's a good idea.

Silence.

SAMINA   You're looking smart.

SHAZ   Interview. Barclays.

SAMINA   How'd it go?

SHAZ   Alright.

SAMINA   Have you heard anything more about this place?

SHAZ   About what?

SAMINA   When you can open again.

SHAZ   It's over Sammy.

SAMINA   Can't be. It had nothing to do with you/

SHAZ   One of my workers! I employed that piece of shit. It's over! The end!

Beat.

SHAZ   Just pray I get the Barclays job.

SAMINA   InshAllah.

Beat.

SHAZ   Naila rang. Finally.

SAMINA   And?

SHAZ   It's not gonna happen. It's over as well. Her dad doesn't want anything to do with us. Naila's tried, but he's not gonna change his mind.

SAMINA	Give him time.
SHAZ	Don't blame him. I'd be the same.
SAMINA	It's only been two weeks.
SHAZ	No point fighting it. Best for us call it a day. Can't be arsed anymore.

Beat.

SAMINA	I'm sorry bhai.

SCENE 14

About two months later. October 20th. Midland Hotel in Bradford City Centre. A 'Bradford for Peace' gathering has just finished at which there has been a number of speakers, including Samina and Andy, who organized the event. Shaz and Faisal were in the audience and are now eating some of the snacks that have been laid out.

SHAZ	Have to say sis, I'm impressed.
SAMINA	Thanks bhai.
FAISAL	Told you she's good at speaking 'n that.
SAMINA	Great turn out, Alhamdulillah. Getting more and more people at every event.
FAISAL	She's got 8,000 followers 'n that!
SAMINA	Yeah my Twitter account's going crazy. A few unsavoury tweets sent my way... but that's to be expected.
SHAZ	Like what?
SAMINA	Retarded Muslims. Saying I'm some kind of traitor to Islam.
SHAZ	Fucking hell.
SAMINA	Keyboard warriors. Think they can say what they want sat in their bedrooms, behind a

computer. If they want a debate, I'll give 'em a debate. Wipe the floor with 'em!

Andy approaches, holding a very large old 80s style camcorder.

ANDY	Hello mate. Assalaamu-alaycum as they say.
SHAZ	Wa-alaycum-assalaam.
ANDY	You must be her brother I take it?
SHAZ	I am yeah.
ANDY	She's a good 'un this one. Although we have our healthy disagreements sometimes.
SAMINA	Not so much now.
ANDY	Had a BBC documentary film-maker in.
SAMINA	Really?!
ANDY	Mentioned he'd like to make a documentary about us.
SAMINA	Oh my god!
ANDY	Gave me his card.

He passes her a business card.

SAMINA	I'll have to discuss it with my brother obviously.
ANDY	Yeah do that. Good job I had this baby *(the camcorder)* with me. Showed him some footage. Seemed very keen.
FAISAL	Is it gonna be on the TV n' that?!
SAMINA	Yeah.
FAISAL	That'd be wicked man!
ANDY	Guess who else came?
SAMINA	Who?
ANDY	Mariam.

SAMINA	That's amazing Andy.
ANDY	She's outside waiting for me. Better go.
SAMINA	Good luck.
ANDY	Thanks. *(To Shaz and Faisal)* Good to meet you.
SHAZ	You too mate.
ANDY	See ya.
SAMINA	See ya Andy.
FAISAL	See ya!

Andy exits.

SAMINA	I'm so touched you came bhai.
SHAZ	Yeah.
SAMINA	Thought any more about the garage?
SHAZ	Twenty-four seven.
SAMINA	And?
SHAZ	It was good the police closed it down for a while. Gave me some time to think.
SAMINA	Been thinking for two months. You're free to open again. You had regular customers.
SHAZ	They'll never come back. No workers now anyway. This fella's off in a few weeks.
FAISAL	I'm not going bro.
SHAZ	What?
FAISAL	Told ma dad 'no'.
SHAZ	How'd he take it?
FAISAL	Pretty bad. Very bad actually. But my cousin isn't fat enough!

SHAZ *(laughs)* Fuckin' hell Fes!

FAISAL	But seriously bro. I saw this premises on Great Horton Road for sale 'n that. We

	could buy it! Start up again! From scratch! Just me and you! Make it a success!
SHAZ	Not a bad idea actually. Different location.
SAMINA	Sounds like a bloody good idea to me.
FAISAL	Shall we check it out bro?!
SHAZ	I'll think about it.
FAISAL	Well don't think too long coz I'll get a job at Kwik-Fit 'n that!!
SHAZ	You alright, Fes?
FAISAL	Yeah!!
SHAZ	Have you taken summat?
FAISAL	Red Bull. Five cans.
SAMINA	What?!
FAISAL	Needed it. To face ma dad.
SHAZ	No wonder. Hyper as fuck.
FAISAL	Slightly sick as well.
SAMINA	Hey, so you're both single right?
FAISAL	Yeah. You can find someone better than that Naila.
SHAZ	Not sure about that.
SAMINA	There's a crappy Muslim speed-dating event in here next week.
SHAZ	No chance.
FAISAL	I'll do it!
SHAZ	I know *you* will, Fes.
SAMINA	Worth a try though. For a laugh.
SHAZ	Maybe. InshAllah.

The End.